Englisch lernen mit 

Rachel Gibson

Now and Forever

Berlitz Publishing
München • New York • Singapur

Berlitz Englisch lernen mit Rachel Gibson
Now and Forever

Vokabelerklärungen und Übungen: Johanna Ellsworth
Lektorat: Christiane Heil
Layout: Ute Weber
Cover-Gestaltung: Dominik Lommer
Projektleitung: Eva Betz

Berlitz Publishing
Mies-van-der-Rohe-Straße 1
D-80807 München

Satz: Franzis print & media GmbH, München
Druck: Mercedes-Druck, Berlin
Printed in Germany
ISBN 978-3-468-79246-5

10010

Inhalt

Liebe Leserin, lieber Leser,

mit dem unterhaltsamen Kurzroman von Rachel Gibson halten Sie endlich ein Englischbuch in der Hand, das Sie garantiert nicht mehr weglegen wollen. Und vor lauter Spannung und Gefühl merken Sie vielleicht gar nicht, dass Sie ganz nebenbei auch Ihre Englischkenntnisse gehörig auffrischen und erweitern.
Damit Ihr Lesevergnügen nicht durch das Nachschlagen unbekannter Wörter gemindert wird, sind die schwierigsten Vokabeln im Text blau markiert und in der Marginalspalte übersetzt. Interessante Wörter, die in einer Infobox erklärt werden, sind zusätzlich mit einem Sternchen gekennzeichnet. Alle übersetzten Wörter sind außerdem im Wörterverzeichnis im Anhang zusammengefasst.
Allein beim Schmökern im Kurzroman können Sie sehr viel dazulernen. Vielleicht möchten Sie aber auch Ihr Grammatikwissen und Ihre Vokabelkenntnisse zusätzlich erweitern oder aber Ihr Textverständnis prüfen. Zu diesem Zweck finden Sie auf jeder Doppelseite knifflige und unterhaltsame Übungen. Die Vokabeln aus dem Text werden dort noch einmal verwendet und bleiben dadurch viel besser im Gedächtnis haften – so können Sie später leichter darauf zurückgreifen. Selbstverständlich sind auch die Lösungen zu allen Übungen im Anhang abgedruckt.

Und nun wünschen wir Ihnen viel Spaß beim Lesen!
Ihre Berlitz-Redaktion

Now and Forever

One

Brina McConnell slid her feet into a pair of five-inch kiss-my-ass high heels and buckled the tiny straps around her ankles. The shoes were red suede and looked like she'd found them in the closet of a well-dressed hooker. Brina loved shoes that boosted her height to a whopping five foot seven. They made her legs look long and lanky – something every short girl dreamed of and tall girls took for granted.

She stood and, with the ease of a woman accustomed to balancing her weight on spiky heels and chunky wedgies, she walked to the mirror. She placed her hand over the butterflies in her stomach and eyed herself critically from the tip of her shoes to the top of her dark hair. The itinerary had indicated semiformal dress for the cocktail party, and Brina's sleeveless red dress was perfect. It was simple and basic and hugged the curves that had developed only after high school. Her chocolate brown hair curled softly to the middle of her back, and she'd painted her lips a deep red and lined her hazel eyes with a kohl pencil. She looked dramatic and a bit exotic, and most of the time she was pleased with the woman she'd become. But not tonight. Tonight when she looked at herself, she saw the flat-chested skinny teenager her classmates had called "munchkin." Of course, that had only been when they'd remembered her at all. Most of the time they'd just ignored her like she hadn't even existed.

Brina moved to the bedside table and reached for the itinerary that had been sent to her office in Portland. The words *Galliton High School Class of 1990 Reunion* were embossed across the top of the page. The weekend's events were listed below, starting with

ließ … gleiten • du-kannst-mich-mal • Pumps • machte … zu • Riemen • Wildleder • Kleiderschrank • Nutte • gigantisch • ein Meter siebzig • schlaksig • klobig • Keilabsätze • Programm

schmiegte sich an die Rundungen

Kajalstift

dürr • Zwerg

Klassentreffen • geprägt

tonight's cocktail party and dance. The reunion committee had planned ski events and a tour of the old high school tomorrow afternoon, followed by a big New Year's Eve celebration tomorrow night. The reunion ended with Sunday's brunch.

Silvesterparty

Brina wasn't surprised that the high school reunion committee had chosen to hold the reunion the weekend of the New Year instead of a more traditional summer month. The small town of Galliton Pass revolved around the ski season, and with not much more to recommend it but the promise of the country's best packed powder, the town all but shut down during the summer. In an effort to draw as many tourist dollars as possible, New Year's Eve in Galliton Pass had always been a huge event.

drehte sich um

Pulverschnee • die Stadt war so gut wie ausgestorben • einzunehmen • sich zu versammeln

In the ballroom somewhere below, Brina's classmates had already begun to assemble for the past half hour. There'd been 78 members of her graduating class*, and she wondered how many had showed.

One person she knew hadn't made the trip was her best friend since the ninth grade, Stephanie. Stephanie now lived in East Texas and had just given birth to her second baby girl. No way would she leave a newborn, and bringing a tiny baby all the way to Galliton

neunte Klasse

info

Die US-amerikanische high school schließt mit der 12. Klasse ab und ist in etwa mit der Gesamtschule in Deutschland vergleichbar. Ein Jahrgang ist nicht in die Klassen a bis d unterteilt; wie an deutschen Universitäten wählen die Schüler der high school ihre Fächer selbst, stellen sich so ihren Stundenplan zusammen und besuchen ihre Fächer in den dafür zugeteilten Klassenzimmern. Brinas Abschlussklasse besteht daher aus ihrem gesamten Jahrgang von 78 Schülern.

Nach dem Besuch der Grundschule (elementary school, primary school, grade school) wechseln alle amerikanischen Schüler für die Sekundarbildung auf die weiterführende high school, deren Abschluss zum Besuch eines junior college qualifiziert.

wasn't an option Stephanie would ever even consider. Not to visit a bunch of kids who'd pretty much ignored her too.

In Galliton Pass there really wasn't much of a middle class. It was filled with the haves and have-nots, and there weren't many in between. There were those who owned businesses in the resort town, and those who worked for them. Brina and her friends belonged to the latter.

The paper fell from her hand to the hotel bed. She was stalling and knew it. She was a private investigator with the firm of Cane, Foster and Morgan. In her professional life, she traced missing people who didn't want to be found, and she uncovered facts that were best left buried. In the beginning she'd investigated a lot of cheating cases, but now she mostly spent her days searching for missing people and things, or she investigated insurance fraud. On more than one occasion she'd proved she was just as tough as any man. She'd had to get really ballsy while going toe to toe with biological parents who didn't want to pay their child support, or spouses who wanted to remain missing.

Brina reached for her red silk shawl and wrapped it around her elbows. It had taken coming home to make

Haufen

den Reichen und den Armen • Ferienort

den Letzteren • zögerte • Privatdetektivin

spürte … Vermisste auf • verborgen • Fälle von Betrug

Versicherungsbetrug • mutig • gegenübertrat • Ehepartner

Das US-Schulsystem ist weitaus freier als das deutsche und legt Wert auf die Förderung von kreativen Begabungen (Theaterkurse, kreatives Schreiben, Kunst, Werken, politische Debatten, Rhetorik, Sport).

Übung 1

Bitte setzen Sie die richtigen Buchstaben und Satzzeichen in die Lücken ein.

The itin__r__ry had indi__ated se__iformal dress for the cockt__il party__ and Brina__s sle__veles__ red dress was perfe__t.

her feel insecure and unsure of herself, but she'd had to come. She had to show them that she was somebody. That she wasn't the insignificant girl who would have done just about anything to be included. The girl who'd lost something important when she'd tried.

She grabbed her little silk purse, and without pausing to check her flaws one last time in the mirror, she walked out of Room 316 and into the hall of Timber Creek Lodge. She rode the elevator to the first floor, and as soon as the doors opened, she heard the party down the hall to her left. To her right, skiers relaxed in the lounge around a big fire.

Seidentäschchen • Fehler • (Name des Hotels, etwa „Holzbach-Hotel")

Brina took a left to the registration table. The line had dwindled except for a man and his very pregnant wife, and she waited for them to move on before she stepped forward and looked into the eyes of Mindy Franklin, head cheerleader and class secretary. Mindy was still cute in a perky sort of way, like she could still jump up and demand everyone show their school spirit. Only now her name tag read Mindy Burton. She'd obviously married her high school sweetheart, president of the ski team and future heir to Timber Creek Lodge, Brett Burton.

die Schlange hatte sich aufgelöst

Haupt- • auf eine quirlige Art süß • Namensschild • Freund • • zukünftiger Erbe

Übung 2 Welche Aussagen sind richtig? Bitte kreuzen Sie die korrekten Aussagen an.

- ☐ Brina has long brown hair.
- ☐ She is usually not pleased with the way she looks.
- ☐ She is flat-chested and skinny.
- ☐ Brina works in Portland.
- ☐ The school reunion will be over Sunday night.
- ☐ The small town of Galliton Pass is a summer resort.
- ☐ Brina comes from a rich family.
- ☐ Brina's friend Stephanie stayed at home with her baby.
- ☐ Brina is a police investigator.

"Your name?"

Brina didn't expect her to remember. Since graduation, she'd grown two inches taller, a full cup size bigger, and finally developed a butt. "Brina McConnell."

Mindy's mouth fell open. "Brina McConnell? I wouldn't have recognized you."

"I was a late bloomer."

"You're not the only one. Wait until you see Thomas Mack." Mindy handed Brina a name tag. "But you probably see him all the time. Wasn't he your boyfriend?"

Yes, for a short time Thomas Mack had been her boyfriend, but before that, they'd been friends since the first grade. An image flashed across her mind of a boy with big blue eyes and long black lashes. He'd always been tall for his age, so skinny his bones stuck out, and so damn smart he'd been offered scholarships from the top universities in the country.

She pinned her name tag to her dress and answered, "No, I haven't seen Thomas since twelfth grade." Not since she'd dumped him their senior year for Mark Harris, quarterback and all-around popular muscle neck.

For eleven years she and Thomas had been close friends. For six months in the summer and fall of 1989, they'd been more, but for the last ten years, they hadn't spoken. Not since the night she'd gone to his house to tell him Mark Harris had asked her to the Christmas prom, and she'd said yes. She'd ruined her relationship with Thomas over a guy like Mark. Thank God she'd grown up, and somewhere along the way learned that she was perfectly okay exactly the way she was.

Back then she supposed she'd been a bit starstruck. In a town the size of Galliton, the quarterback of the football team was a local celebrity, eclipsed only by the captain of the ski team. Mark had been *somebody,* and he'd noticed *her.*

Körbchengröße • Hintern

Spätentwicklerin

Wimpern

Stipendien

fallen ließ • Spielmacher (im American Football) • allgemein

Schulball

von seinem Ruhm geblendet • Berühmtheit • übertroffen

She hadn't wanted to hurt Thomas, hadn't wanted to lose him, and she'd gone to his house that night hoping they could remain friends. She should have known better. The night she'd broken up with him, he'd looked at her through eyes turned cold and had said, "You always did want to sit at the big table. Here's your chance. Just don't expect me to pick up the pieces. I won't be around." And he hadn't been. Exactly one month later, Mark had dumped her flat, and Thomas had moved on. After that, whenever they'd been in the same room, he'd looked at her as if she were a stranger.

"I guess he's really successful now."

"Who?"

"Thomas Mack. He started a computer software company. I heard he recently sold it for millions."

Good, Brina thought. Thomas had always boasted that he'd be a millionaire by the time he was thirty. It sounded as if he'd done it. One of the outcasts, a guy whose parents had been killed when he'd been a baby. A boy who'd been raised by grandparents who'd loved him, but had little money to provide for a child, had made it big. It would be good to see him again.

"I'm sure I'll see you around," Brina said, and walked into the ballroom.

The room was decorated with white streamers, and white balloons lay strewn about on the floor. On the far side, a stage had been erected and was swathed with white bunting and silver glitter. A band had set up their instruments, but for now the stage was empty. On a dozen or so easels about the room sat different blown-up photos of the class of 1990. Crowds had gathered at each easel and were reliving their high school glory days. Brina didn't bother to look at the pictures. She knew she probably wasn't in any of them.

The huge floor-to-ceiling windows and doors on the left side of the room led out to a deck and overlooked a ski run thick with moguls and aptly named "Show-

an dem Abend, an dem sie mit ihm Schluss gemacht hatte • die Scherben aufzusammeln • eiskalt

damit geprahlt

Außenseiter

um für ein Kind zu sorgen • hatte es zu etwas gebracht

• Luftschlangen • verstreut • überhäuft • Fähnchen

Staffeleien • vergrößert

Terrasse • Skipiste • Buckel • passend

boat." The glass reflected wavy images of the people inside, and if Brina looked hard enough toward the top, she could see that it was snowing outside.

She made her way through the round tables set up on the perimeter and spotted several faces she recognized. At the bar, she ordered a gin and tonic and glanced about the room, searching for a tall gangly man with unruly hair. Her gaze skimmed from table to table, then stopped dead on a group standing near the champagne fountain. She knew them from band class. All except one.

As if he felt her gaze on him, the man she didn't recognize turned his head and looked at her, and a little tingle joined the butterflies in her stomach.

His dark hair was cut short, and unlike some of the men around him, he looked like he would still need a comb for many years to come. She couldn't see the color of his eyes, but they were deep set and a bit intense as he stared back at her. His cheeks were wide, his jaw perfectly square, and his deep blue suit fit his broad shoulders with the flawless tailoring that could only come from a designer label. One side of the jacket was brushed back, and he'd shoved a hand in the pocket of his trousers. His white shirt fit flat against

gewellt

Peripherie • entdeckte • schlaksig • widerspenstig • blieb abrupt … hängen

Kribbeln

Kiefer • makellos • Schnitt • zurückgeschoben • gesteckt

Übung 3

Welches Wort passt nicht in die Wortgruppe?
Bitte unterstreichen Sie es.

1. husband, wife, marriage, spouse
2. photo, picture, drawing, vision
3. blackboard, teacher, pupil, graduate
4. suit, purse, jacket, trousers
5. insured, unsure, insecure, sure
6. jaw, flaw, butt, cheek
7. unruly, gangly, really, wavy

Brustkorb • Nadel • frech • glitt • verharrte • reuelos • bewundernd • sie hätte fast die Limettenscheibe … eingesogen • korrigierte sie sich • muskulös • als hätte sie selbst nicht genug vorzuweisen • sofort • rotbraun

his chest, and his blue tie was held in place by a thin gold clasp.

Brina raised her glass to her lips. Some lucky girl's husband, she thought, until his bold gaze slid over her, touching her lips and throat and lingering over her breasts. Normally, she probably would have been offended by his unrepentant staring, but it didn't feel as if he were looking at her with sexual interest. More out of mild curiosity, as if he were inspecting her instead of checking her out. But when his eyes moved to her hips and legs, then began the slow process all the way back up, an appreciative smile curved the corners of his mouth, and she about sucked in the lime slice from her drink.

Perhaps not a husband after all, she amended. Probably some girl had begged a hunky guy to escort her tonight. Or hired an underwear model. Brina had thought of that too, but in the end she hadn't because it made her feel as if she wasn't okay by herself.

"Brina McConnell?"

Brina tore her attention from the man across the room and looked at the woman in front of her. Instantly she recognized the light green eyes and long auburn hair. "Karen Johnson, how are you?"

Übung 4 Die folgenden Sätze sind durcheinandergeraten. Bitte setzen Sie die Wörter in die richtige Reihenfolge.

1. her was checking her instead of inspecting he out

____

____

2. in the gold clasp was place held by a blue tie

____

____

3. gotten wine on Karen's daddy's they'd homemade drunk

____

____

She and Karen had been president and vice president of The Future Homemakers of America together, and they'd gotten drunk on Karen's daddy's homemade wine on more than one occasion.

Hausfrauen

Karen spread her arms wide, then laid her hand on her very rounded tummy. "Pregnant with my third," she said.

Bauch • schwanger

Third? Brina had only had two serious relationships since high school, and neither had lasted more than a few years. "Who'd you marry?"

gehalten

"Which time?" Karen laughed.

Brina didn't know how to respond to that. She didn't think "Holy shit" would be appropriate, so she asked instead, "Have you seen Thomas Mack? I heard he's here tonight."

du liebe Scheiße • angebracht

Karen looked around, then pointed directly at the underwear model. "There he is."

* * *

Thomas Mack knew the precise second Brina McConnell realized who he was. Her eyes rounded and her mouth fell open right before he watched her lips form the words, "Oh my God, you're kidding." Before that

das kannst du nicht ernst meinen

4. since Brina had had only two high relationships serious school

____

____

5. neither more relationship lasted than had few years a

____

____

6. reliving were school crowds their high glory days

____

____

7. Brina didn't to look at the pictures bother

____

____

Ahnung • hatte Kurven bekommen • erinnerte sich an • haselnussbraun

moment, she hadn't had a clue. He'd changed since high school and so had she. She'd filled out and grown more beautiful than the girl he'd known.

He recalled the first time he'd seen her on the first day of first grade, and he remembered her big hazel eyes and enormous ponytail. She'd always had such thick hair, it made her head look too big for her neck.

Mandeln • Eis am Stiel • geschmolzen

He also remembered the first time he'd bought her a present. It had been in the third grade, after she'd had her tonsils out. He'd bought her a blue Popsicle that had cost him a quarter and had melted on the way to her house.

Beerdigung • Labrador

He remembered the day his dog, Scooter, had died, the funeral they'd given the old black Lab, and the way he'd held Brina while she'd cried like she was never going to stop. Thomas had been thirteen and hadn't cried, but he'd wanted to. That had also been the day he'd noticed the changes in her body for the first time. He'd been holding her, trying to act like a man and trying not to cry over the loss of his dog. And as he'd stood there, battling himself, her soft hands clutching him through his tank top and her little breasts poking his chest and driving him crazy, he'd tried not to think of her naked. He remembered push-

mit sich kämpfte • umklammerten • stießen gegen

Übung 5 Unterstreichen Sie die jeweils richtige Verbform in Klammern.

1. Brina had (growed / grown / grew) into more of a woman than the girl he'd known.
2. The stranger's eyes (moved / moving / moves) to her hips and legs.
3. Probably some girl had (bagged / begged / bugged) a hunky guy to escort her tonight.
4. "Who (were / does / did) you marry?"
5. He had (buy / bought / buying) her a blue Popsicle that (had / – / has) cost him a quarter.
6. She didn't (knew / know / knows) how to respond to that.

ing her away and telling her to go home because her blubbering was making him feel worse. She'd left angry and never knew that it hadn't been her crying that had made him send her away. It had been the sudden aching thud in his chest, and the pounding in his groin. From that day forward, Brina McConnell had tortured him and hadn't even known it.

It wasn't until the summer going into their senior year of high school that Thomas had decided it was time to do something about his feelings for Brina. They'd been with a group of friends at The Reel To Reel Theater, when he'd leaned over and kissed her for the first time, right in the middle of *Rain Man*. She hadn't been his first girlfriend, but when she'd ended their relationship, she'd been the first girl to knock him flat. It had taken him a year or two and several more girlfriends to get over Brina McConnell.

Since leaving Galliton Pass ten years ago, Thomas had seen and done a lot. He'd earned a full scholarship to Berkeley and had graduated high school with enough advanced placement credits to enter as a sophomore. Three years later, he'd graduated with a double major in finance and computer science. Right out of college, he'd been hired by Microsoft, but he'd quickly discovered that working for someone else wasn't what he wanted. After a short time, he and two of his friends had quit to start their own software company, BizTech. They'd developed programs to predict business and market trends, and in the beginning he'd loved his work. But the bigger the growth, the less he'd enjoyed himself.

The day BizTech went public was the day the company made the Fortune 500. It was also the day he remembered why he'd quit working for Microsoft. The company no longer belonged to him, and worrying about market shares and shareholders wasn't what he wanted to do for the rest of his life. Five months ago he'd sold his interest in the company and gotten out completely.

Flennen

schmerzhaftes Klopfen • Hämmern • Leistengegend • gequält

Kino

das ihn am Boden zerstört zurückließ • um über … hinwegzukommen • (Anrechnung schulischer Leistungen im Studium) • Student im 2. Jahr • doppelter Abschluss • gekündigt • vorauszusagen

je … desto • an die Börse ging • auf die Liste der 500 größten amerikanischen Unternehmen kam • Marktanteile • Aktionäre • Anteil

Thomas was twenty-eight, had enough money to last several lifetimes, and for the first time was without direction or goals. He understood completely the stories he read about doctors and lawyers who closed successful practices to become cowboys and race car drivers. While herding cattle and racing cars didn't appeal to him, he had given some thought to doing consultant work. He wasn't certain what he wanted to do now, but he had time to figure it out.

George Allen, surgical supply salesman and former first-seat trombonist and class comedian, cracked a joke and everyone around him laughed.

Ziele • Vieh zusammenzutreiben • beratende Tätigkeit • Operationszubehör • Posaunist • riss einen Witz

All of his life Thomas had worked hard to succeed, and he'd never looked back. Not until he'd opened the notice to his high school reunion. When he'd first read Brina's name on the list of attendees, he'd been a little curious about her. He'd wondered if she'd gone to fat or had five kids. The more he'd wondered, the more his curiosity had gotten the better of him.

Ankündigung • Teilnehmende

If he was completely honest with himself, part of the reason he was here tonight was that he wanted to stand back and see if Brina still made his chest get tight when he looked at her. If the sight of her brought a lump to his throat.

She didn't.

He raised his drink and watched Brina over the rim of his glass. She leaned to the left and looked around Karen Johnson's hair. Then she smiled, a purely feminine tilt of her mouth that had tortured him from grade eight clear through twelve. A female mystery of softly parted lips that used to make him suck in his breath and left his hands aching to touch her. He remembered the times in her room or his house or sitting in his grandmother's old Reliant, when he'd been so hard he'd wondered what she'd do if she knew. If he took her hand and let her feel what she did to him. She'd driven him bleary eyed with lust, and he'd never done much more than kiss her.

einen Kloß im Hals • Rand • Verziehen • (Automarke; meist Dreiradfahrzeuge) • seine Augen hatten sich vor Verlangen nach ihr getrübt

Thomas polished off his drink as George told another joke, this one concerning women and fish, and again Thomas was the only person who didn't laugh. He didn't need to beat his chest or degrade anyone to feel like a man. He might not have lost his virginity until his first year of college, but he'd made up for lost time, and he could honestly say he'd never been with a woman who smelled like a fish. Laughing would imply that he had, and frankly, it made him wonder about the caliber of women George knew.

leerte

sich ... an die Brust zu schlagen • zu erniedrigen • Unschuld • aufgeholt • suggerieren • ehrlich gesagt

"Talk to you later," he said, and made his way to the bar. Some people might think he didn't have a sense of humor. He did, but growing up, he'd been the butt of too many belittling jokes to laugh at them now.

Sinn • Zielscheibe • herabsetzend

He ordered a scotch and water, then turned, and his gaze landed on Brina, who'd moved to stand right in front of him. The top of her head reached his mouth, and he looked down into the greenish gray eyes he remembered so well.

"Hey there, Thomas," she said.

Her voice didn't sound the same. It was lower, feminine. More like a woman than a girl. "Hello, Brina."

"Are you here alone tonight?"

Übung 6

Ordnen Sie die Wortpaare, die zusammengehören, einander zu.

1. lawyer	☐ family
2. driver	☐ product
3. consultant	☐ clothing
4. doctor	☐ music
5. investigator	☐ race car
6. homemaker	☐ justice
7. trombonist	☐ patient
8. salesman	☐ advice
9. teacher	☐ crime
10. model	☐ student

"Tonight and the whole weekend." He'd thought about bringing a woman. His last girlfriend had modeled lingerie for Victoria's Secret. They were still on friendly terms, and she probably would have come with him if he'd asked.

Unterwäsche

"Thank God," she sighed on a breathless little laugh. "I thought I was going to be the only single person here."

"George Allen is here alone."

"Unless he's changed a lot, I'm not surprised." She shook her head. "You look good, Thomas. I didn't recognize you right away."

He'd recognized her the second she'd walked in the room. "I changed after high school."

in dem Moment

"Me too. I grew two inches."

That wasn't all she'd grown, and Thomas purposely kept his eyes pinned to her face rather than run them up and down her body again. Which was exactly what he wanted to do. Not that he felt lust for her anymore, but he was still curious. That growing streak she'd mentioned had popped out a nice set of breasts, and out of curiosity, he wouldn't mind stripping off her dress and taking a really close look. His brows lowered and he tried to think of something else. The weather. World politics. Who would win the Stanley Cup this season? Anything besides undressing the only woman who'd ripped his heart out.

bewusst

Wachstumsschub • hervorgebracht

(Trophäe im Eishockey) • die ihm das Herz gebrochen hatte

Two

Brina studied Thomas's serious blue eyes and tilted her head. Except for the color of his hair and eyes, this man standing in front of her didn't much resemble the skinny boy from her past. "I don't know if you know this," she said in an effort at conversation, "but everyone is talking about you tonight."

musterte • legte den Kopf schräg

ähnelte • Versuch, die Unterhaltung in Gang zu bringen

He lifted a brow. "Really? What are they saying?"

"You don't know?"

He shook his head and took a drink.

"Well," she began, "it's going around that you're richer than Donald Trump, and you're dating Elle Macpherson and Kathy Ireland at the same time."

"I must be better than I thought." For the first time since Brina had seen him that night, the corners of his deep blue eyes hinted that he might be amused. "But I'm sorry to disappoint everyone," he said. "None of that is true."

(US-amerik. Milliardär) • (austral. Fotomodell) • (US-amerik. Fotomodell)

Übung 7

Setzen Sie die Substantive in die jeweils passende Lücke:
second, conversation, laugh, humor, lingerie, drink, chest

1. Thomas polished off his ________________.
2. He didn't need to beat his ________________.
3. He just had a different sense of ________________.
4. His former girlfriend modeled ________________ for an American company.
5. Thomas spotted Brina the ________________ she walked into the room.
6. Brina sighed a breathless little ________________.
7. Then she made an effort at ________________.

"Hmm." She took a drink. "That means the other rumor probably isn't true either."

"Which is?"

"The worse thing you can be in this town."

A corner of his mouth lifted. "Someone said I'm gay?"

"No, worse. They say you've turned Democrat."

He smiled then. It started with the slow curving of his lips and slid into full-fledged pleasure. "God forbid." He laughed, at first hesitant, then a rich masculine sound deep from in his chest that stirred the butterflies in her stomach and fluttered across her skin like the slightest touch. "I wouldn't want the local NRA to come gunning for me."

The humor crinkling the corners of his eyes transformed his face from merely handsome to check-for-drool devastating. "No," Brina uttered as she ran her gaze down his straight nose to the deep furrow molding the bow in his top lip. "You wouldn't want that."

"How's your family?" he asked.

"Good," she managed, and looked into his eyes once again. She'd dumped this guy for Mark Harris. What in the hell had she been thinking? "None of us live around here anymore. How are your grandparents?"

Gerücht

schwul

geriet zu • richtig • Gott behüte! • aufwirbelte • flatterte • die hiesige Waffenlobby • mich verfolgt • der … in Fältchen legte • einfach nur gut aussehend • zum Sabbern umwerfend • Furche • die … formte • Kurve

Übung 8 Welche Gegensätze bilden ein Paar?

1. effort		dress
2. tuxedo		former
3. rumor		back
4. Democrat		discomfort
5. hell		criminal
6. latter		Republican
7. funeral		heaven
8. investigator		fact
9. pleasure		ease
10. chest		birth

"Getting older. I moved them to Palm Springs for their health. They didn't like it at first, but now they love it." He raised his glass and took a drink. "Where do you live these days?"

"Portland," she answered, and while she told him about her work, she searched his face and couldn't help but look for any trace of the boy she'd known. Physically there was very little resemblance. His eyes were still dark blue and his lashes thick. His cheeks were no longer hollow and his dark hair was cut short to the tops of his ears, the unruly waves tamed.

Spur • Ähnlichkeit

hohl

gezähmt

When her gaze returned to his, he asked, "What are you looking for, Brina?"

"You," she answered. "I'm wondering if I know you anymore."

"I doubt it."

"That's too bad. Do you remember the summer we spent hunting witches and vampires in the forest?"

Hexen zu jagen

"No."

"We made spears and wooden crosses."

Speere •

"That's right. I remember," he said as the chandeliers in the ballroom dimmed, and they turned their attention to the stage. When the spotlight hit the white bunting and silver glitter, it suddenly looked like the first winter snow.

Kronleuchter

"Hi everyone, I'm Mindy Franklin Burton," Mindy announced from behind the podium. "Welcome to the Galliton Pass class of 1990 high school reunion." Everyone clapped except Brina. She couldn't. She had a glass in her hand. She looked to her left. Thomas didn't applaud either. And suddenly she wondered why Thomas was here. For as long as she could remember, he'd always said that when he left Galliton, he was never coming back. The one time she'd asked if he would come back and see her, he'd told her she could come with him.

"In 1990, we listened to Robert Palmer, New Kids on the Block, and U2," Mindy continued.

Not Thomas, Brina remembered. He'd listened to Bob Dylan and Eric Clapton.

"George Bush was sworn in as the forty-first president and Lucille Ball died at the age of seventy-seven. On television we watched 'Cheers' and 'L.A. Law,' and when we went to the theater, we saw *Arachnaphobia* and *Ghost*. And in our own …"

vereidigt

Brina's thoughts returned to the tall man wearing the impeccably tailored suit standing beside her, and she again wondered why he'd returned after vowing so often that he would not. Perhaps, like her, he'd come here to show everyone that he wasn't insignificant, that he'd made a success of his life, but Thomas had never cared what any of them thought. In fact, she'd never known a person who cared so little about impressing anyone, but it had been ten years. People changed. She certainly had, and he had to have changed too.

makellos • zugeschnitten • er … geschworen hatte

zu beeindrucken

"In 1990," Mindy continued, "our football team took state, and our ski team took first place in the all-around events."

gewann die Bundesstaatsmeisterschaften

The cell phone in the inside pocket of Thomas's jacket chirped, and he reached his hand in and pulled it out. In a low hushed voice, he spoke into the phone. "How are you feeling? … What did he say? … Oh …" There was a pause, then his brows pulled together. "Did you hook it into the serial port like I told you to? … Yeah, that one … Grandmother spilled her Postum in the keyboard? Of course that's a problem … What? Hold on a minute." He looked at Brina. "I'm sure I'll see you before the weekend is over," he said, and then with his drink in one hand, phone in the other, he walked from the ballroom.

• Handy • zwitscherte • gedämpft

angeschlossen • verschüttete • (Ersatzkaffee aus Getreide)

Brina returned her gaze to the stage. The last time she'd been in the ballroom of the Timber Creek Lodge had been the night of the Christmas prom. She'd worn red that night, too. A red satin dress her mother had made for her from material they'd bought from Judy's Fabric Land. She'd worn roses in her hair, and her date, Mark Harris, had worn a black tuxedo.

Brina had had a crush on Mark for years, but it hadn't been until his girlfriend, prom queen and pep club president Holly Buchanan, had dumped him – two weeks before the dance – that he'd taken notice of her and asked her to the prom. They'd dated for a few weeks more, then Holly had snapped her fingers and Mark had gone running back. Brina had been crushed.

As if thinking about him made him appear, Mark Harris stepped in front of her. He looked at her name badge, then smiled. "Munchkin?"

She frowned and he tilted his head back and laughed. He'd always had the straightest white teeth she'd ever seen, and in the past ten years, he hadn't changed much. His blonde hair had turned light brown and he had a few creases at the corners of his green eyes, and if anything, he'd grown more handsome with age. The green of his tie matched his shirt, tucked into a pair of khaki-colored pants. He wasn't as muscular as she remembered, but he still looked fairly buff.

Stoff • Textil • Smoking • war … verknallt • Anfeuerungsklub

mit den Fingern geschnippt • am Boden zerstört

runzelte die Stirn

in … gestopft

fit

Wie lauten die zu diesen Verben passenden Substantive? **Übung 9**

1. to transform __________
2. to disappoint __________
3. to think __________
4. to resemble __________
5. to return __________
6. to remember __________
7. to announce __________
8. to care __________
9. to impress __________
10. to enjoy __________

Mindy continued to speak, the room applauded something she said, and Mark Harris grabbed Brina's shoulders and looked deep into her eyes. "God, you look great," he said through his perfect smile. "I can't believe I dumped you for Holly. I must have been a moron."

It was so close to what she'd been thinking about Thomas that she laughed. "You were, but don't be too hard on yourself. Holly was a walking, talking Malibu Barbie doll." She shook her head. "I always thought the two of you would get married."

"We did. Then we got divorced." He said it as if it were no big deal, and Brina wondered how many other classmates had married and divorced.

"Are you here alone?" he asked.

"Yes."

"What luck. Me too." His smile spread to his eyes. "Come on, let's go talk to some of the guys. Everyone's dying to know who you are, but no one guessed right." He placed a hand in the small of her back and explained. "No one recognized you when you walked in. Then we saw you talking to Thomas Mack and thought you might be his date. You're not, are you?"

grabbed: packte • moron: Idiot • don't be too hard on yourself: geh nicht zu streng mit dir um • Malibu: (schicker Badeort in Kalifornien) • divorced: geschieden • no big deal: keine große Sache • spread: kroch … hinauf • 's dying to know: will unbedingt wissen • guessed right: hat es erraten • in the small of her back: auf ihr Kreuz

Übung 10 Finden Sie mithilfe der Definition das gesuchte Wort im Buchstabensalat.

1. completely faultless (pimaceblec) ____________________

2. your peers in school (ctlemasass) ____________________

3. a place to stay on your winter holidays (dogel) ____________

4. carrying an unborn baby (nptragen) ________________

5. second-year college student (morehoops) ____________

6. an insurance crime (rufda) ____________________

7. no longer married (vedordci) ____________________

8. inofficial law (tutenwirn lure) ____________________

"No." Brina glanced around the room and spied Thomas in the entrance, talking to a tall blonde woman in a tight black dress. There was no mistaking Holly Buchanan, prom queen. From as far back as Brina could remember, Holly had been blonde and beautiful. She'd never gone through an awkward or ugly stage, and if there was an unwritten rule somewhere that stated beautiful rich girls had to be gracious and kind, Holly had never read it. Or perhaps she had and just didn't care.

Thomas and Holly stood in profile to the room, and she placed her hand on the arm of his jacket and smiled up at him. Brina wondered what he'd said to make Holly smile. He hadn't made any effort to make *her* smile. Not even a little. In fact, he'd seemed a bit stiff and uptight. Not at all like the Thomas she remembered.

"I think we're all supposed to be listening to Mindy," she said as Mark directed her to a small group of people to her right. There had been a time when the touch of his hand would have given her heart palpitations. Now he was just someone she used to know, and one of those guys she was eternally grateful she'd never slept with.

spied: entdeckte • There was no mistaking: es war eindeutig • an awkward or ugly stage: eine Phase der Unsicherheit oder Hässlichkeit • gracious: liebenswürdig • made any effort: sich keine Mühe gegeben • stiff: steif • uptight: verkrampft • we're all supposed: wir sollen alle • directed: führte • heart palpitations: Herzklopfen • eternally grateful: ewig dankbar

Übung 11

Beantworten Sie bitte die Fragen zum Text in ganzen Sätzen.

1. What did Holly have to do to get Mark back?

____

____

2. What does Mark call himself for dumping Brina ten years ago?

____

____

3. How does Brina describe the old Holly to Mark?

____

____

"No one listens to Mindy. Not even Brett," he said as he led her to a group of his friends. In school, they'd been the group of kids with money. The group who'd worn their season ski passes on their ski jackets like status symbols because they could. Brina recognized a few of them; others she hadn't clue a about until she was reintroduced. Living in such a small town, she'd grown up with them, but they'd never been her friends.

wieder vorgestellt

Listening to them now, she discovered that most of the people she'd graduated with still lived in the area. Many of them had married right out of high school or college but had quickly divorced and were now on their second and even third relationship. And as they talked about 1990 as if it were the best year of their lives, Brina glanced beyond them to Thomas.

über sie hinweg

High school hadn't been the high point of her life so far, and it hadn't been the high point of his either. As if he read her thoughts, he looked over the top of Holly's head and his gaze met hers. He stared at her for several long seconds, his expression unreadable, then a furrow wrinkled his brow and he looked away.

The lights dimmed even further as Mindy finished with her speech, and Brina could no longer see

Übung 12 Bitte korrigieren Sie die folgenden Sätze im Hinblick auf Satzzeichen und Groß- und Kleinschreibung.

1. when her gaze returned to his he asked what are you looking for Brina
2. you she answered im wondering if I know you anymore
3. everyone clapped except brina she couldnt she had a glass in her hand thomas didnt applaud either
4. george bush was sworn in as the forty first president and lucille ball died at the age of seventy seven mindy continued
5. with his drink in one hand phone in the other thomas left

Thomas's face. He became just an outline in the darkening room.

The band took the stage, thumped and tuned for a moment or two, then started the evening out with a fairly decent rendering of "Turn You Inside Out." Mark grasped Brina's hand and led her onto the dance floor. As he took her in his arms and folded her against his chest, he asked, "What are you doing later?"

Her flight had gotten in late, and she hadn't really thought of anything beyond taking a shower and going to bed. "Going to my room."

"Some of us are going to my house in a while. You should come with us."

She pulled back and looked up into his face. She thought about it and thought she'd rather sleep than listen to more stories about the time Mark and his friends had all skied naked, or the time they'd pranked the Chess Club and hidden all the kings. "I think I'm just going to crash tonight," she said.

"Okay, then meet us tomorrow. We'll be on the back side."

Living so many years in Galliton, she knew he meant that they'd all be skiing the back side of Silver Dollar Mountain. But just because she'd been raised in a resort town didn't mean she knew how to ski. She didn't. "I'll try."

Mark pulled her closer and she looked beyond him and spotted Thomas through the shadows of shifting bodies.

"Your hair smells nice," Mark complimented her.

"Thank you." Thomas held Holly within his embrace, and he moved with a perfect and fluid rhythm she'd never known he possessed. Holly's arms were wound around his neck, and he held her much too close. The sight of his hands resting in the small of her back, their bodies touching, bothered Brina more than it should.

Mark talked about the businesses he owned and he complimented Brina repeatedly. He was charming and

Umriss • trommelten herum und stimmten ihre Instrumente • anständig • Version • sie an seine Brust drückte

einen Streich gespielt hatten • Schachklub • ins Bett fallen

sich bewegender

Umarmung • flüssig • geschlungen

amiable, but her attention was focused on the couple across the dance floor. Her head was filled with their image and her own riotous thoughts, and she wondered why the sight of Thomas and Holly should eat at her. Why it should burn a hole in her stomach.

The answer came to her as the last strains of a guitar echoed in the ballroom. She felt ownership over Thomas as if he were hers. He'd been her good friend for a lot of years, and even though she'd treated him badly toward the end, she still felt a connection to him. And to be completely honest, she hated the sight of him with Holly. Perhaps because she knew that if Thomas were a bus driver or a mechanic, Holly probably wouldn't have crossed the room to speak to him, but there was more to it. More she couldn't explain. More that felt a bit like jealousy. Her feelings didn't make a lot of sense. They weren't logical, but that didn't stop them from twisting her into a confused knot.

She excused herself from Mark and wound her way to the bar. Feeling a little ragged, she wondered if she should order another drink or just go to bed. She did neither. Instead, she ran into her tenth-grade lab partner, Jen Larkin. Jen had packed on about eighty pounds and she still had the most freckles Brina had seen on a person. They chatted for a bit, but the music made conversation near impossible, and mostly the two ended up yelling questions at each other. She lost sight of Thomas through several songs and couldn't help but wonder if he'd sneaked off to jump the prom queen.

He hadn't. He and Holly walked past her and stood in the short line at the bar. Begrudgingly she had to admit that they made a good-looking couple.

From the stage, the band broke into a song Brina recognized from having spent so many years listening to Thomas's cheap stereo. Before she could talk herself out of it, she walked up to him and said, "They're playing our song."

liebenswürdig • konzentrierte sich auf • auf der anderen Seite • aufständisch • an ihr nagen • Melodie • Besitzrechte • innere Verbundenheit

Automechaniker

Eifersucht

sie völlig durcheinander und verwirrt machten • zwängte sich durch • chaotisch • Labor • zugenommen • Sommersprossen • fast • sich davongestohlen • poppen • widerwillig

Stereoanlage • es sich ausreden konnte

Through the dim shadows provided by the chandelier, he looked into Brina's eyes for several long moments as if he were trying to figure something out. Just when she thought he might not say anything at all, he did. "Excuse us, Holly," he said, and took Brina by the elbow. He led her to the middle of the crowded dance floor, then wrapped his warm palm around the back of her left hand. "Since when is 'Lay Lady Lay' our song?" he asked as he grasped her waist.

She placed her hand on his shoulder; the smooth fabric of his jacket felt cool to her touch. "Since you used to make me listen to Bob Dylan for hours."

He glanced over the top of her head. "You hated it."

"No, I just loved to give you a hard time." He held her several inches away from him as if he didn't want her to invade his space. He held her as if he were a dance instructor, moving with perfect impersonal timing. He hadn't minded Holly invading him, though, and she was surprised at how betrayed she felt by that. Her feelings were so crazy, she wondered if she was losing her mind.

"Thomas?"

"Hmm."

für die … sorgte • etwas herauszufinden • Handfläche • glatt • dir das Leben schwer zu machen • es hatte ihm nichts ausgemacht • verraten • ob sie dabei war, den Verstand zu verlieren

Übung 13

Bitte tragen Sie die gesuchten Körperteile auf Englisch ein.

1. The inside of your hand is called your p______________.
2. Please don't dig me in the ribs with your e______________!
3. The stranger's gaze lingered on her big b______________.
4. Thomas held her close to his muscular c______________,
5. She felt butterflies in her s______________.
6. Looking at her, he lifted a b______________.
7. Thomas had beautiful eyes with long black l______________.
8. He put his hand on her s______________ and started to dance with her.

She looked up into the shadows of his face, into the darkness concealing his eyes and outlining his nose and finely etched mouth. "Are you still mad at me?"

die … verbarg • in der sich … abzeichnete • geformt • sauer

Finally he gazed down at her. "No."

"Then do you think we can be friends again?"

As if he had to consider that too, several lines of the song passed before he answered, "What do you have in mind?"

Was stellst du dir vor?

She didn't really know. "Well, what are you doing tomorrow?"

"Skiing."

She was a little surprised by his answer. "When did you learn?"

"About six years ago."

At a loss for witty conversation, she asked, "So do you like it?"

geistreich

His grasp on her waist tightened sightly, and he pulled her a fraction closer. "I have a condo in Aspen," he answered as if that said it all, and perhaps it did.

Spur • Eigentumswohnung • (populärer Wintersportort)

His thumb lightly brushed her palm and he folded their hands into his chest. Pleasurable tingles spread up her wrist and arm, as if chased by a breath of warm air. "Are you skiing with Holly?" she asked as if she weren't dying to know.

• angenehm • Kribbeln

Übung 14

Kreuzen Sie bitte die richtige Antwort an. Es gibt nur jeweils eine richtige Lösung!

1. ________________ was interested in what Mindy had to say.

- ☐ Everyone
- ☐ No one
- ☐ Only Brett
- ☐ Only Brina

2. Brina arrived in Galliton Pass ________________________.

- ☐ in the morning
- ☐ at noon
- ☐ in the afternoon
- ☐ in the evening

"Whoever. Are you going to meet up with Mark Harris and that bunch?"
"No." She didn't want to waste time talking about Mark. "Remember the time I saved all of my baby-sitting money so I could buy equipment and join the Ski Club?"
"You broke your leg the first day."
"Yep. I haven't tried it since." She moved her palm across his shoulder, and she touched the collar of his white shirt. Beneath her sensitive fingertips, his flesh had warmed the thick linen. "I thought I might do some shopping and hang out at the lodge."
His hand slid to the small of her back, and he eased her into the solid wall of his chest. Brina's breath caught in her throat.
"Sounds boring," he said against her right temple, but he didn't offer to keep her company.
"Have you seen all the pregnant women in this room? I'll find someone to talk to." Brina turned her face slightly and breathed deep. She filled her lungs with the scent of his cologne and the warmth of his skin. He smelled so good she was tempted to lean forward and bury her nose in his neck. She lifted her index finger and lightly touched his skin above

Mit wem auch immer. • eine Skiausrüstung • Ja. • Kragen • unter • empfindlich • Leinen • rumhängen • drückte sie sanft an seinen festen Brustkorb • blieb … stecken • Schläfe • ihr Gesellschaft zu leisten • Duft • dass sie versucht war • zu vergraben • Zeigefinger

3. Mark told Brina about the ________________ he owns.

- chess sets
- ski equipment
- businesses
- condos

4. Watching Thomas ________________ with Holly, Brina felt jealous.

- ski
- talk
- dance
- flirt

5. When Brina joined the Ski Club, she ________________.

- broke her leg
- skied naked
- rented her ski equipment
- learned how to ski

his collar. The warmth of his skin tickled her palm.

kitzelte

She wondered what he would do if she told him how much she'd missed him. That she hadn't even realized how much she'd missed him until she'd seen him again tonight, and how genuinely happy she was just to see his face again.

aufrichtig

She wondered if he felt the same, but she was afraid to ask. She wanted to hear about his life. She didn't even know where he lived. "What are you doing for the rest of the night?" she asked, thinking that maybe they could find somewhere and catch up on the last ten years.

aufarbeiten

"I've got a few options, but I'm not sure what I'll do."

She didn't want to look pathetic in front of him, so she said, "Yeah, I have a few options, too. Mark invited me to a party at his house."

lächerlich wirken

The last strains of "Lay Lady Lay" poured from the speakers and Thomas dropped his hands and took a step back.

strömte • Lautsprecher • ließ … sinken

"Maybe we could go together," she offered.

"I don't think so, but thanks." He looked over Brina's head to the tall blonde who stood by the bar where he'd left her. "Holly Buchanan is trying to seduce me," he said. "She's a yoga instructor and says she studies the Kama Sutra."

verführen

"Are you kidding?"

"No. She mentioned something about showing me a goat position."

"That's disturbing." Surely Thomas realized that if he were still poor, Holly wouldn't have uttered a word to him, let alone whispered anything as warped as goat positions in his ear. Thomas couldn't be so stupid as to fall for it. He'd always been too smart. "She's using you."

"Uh huh."

Ziegenstellung • beunruhigend • abartig • darauf hereinzufallen • Sie benutzt dich nur. • Mmh.

"What are you going to do?"

"I think I'll let her."

Three

Brina woke the next morning feeling as tired as when she'd gone to bed. After she'd danced with Thomas, she'd danced with Mark again and had ended up at his house with a bunch of his friends. One thing she'd noticed was that they hadn't evolved that much. Brina had left the party feeling lucky for her life in Portland. She didn't have a boyfriend at the moment, but at least she had a bigger pool to choose from.

When she'd arrived back at her hotel room, she'd crawled into bed only to lie awake all night thinking about Thomas and Holly acting like goats. And the more she'd thought about it, the angrier she'd become until she'd wished Thomas were standing in front of her so she could punch him. She hadn't fallen asleep until around 3:00 A.M. Now it was eight-thirty and she was exhausted.

Brina sat up on the edge of her bed and threw the blankets aside. She dialled room service and ordered a pot of coffee and a toasted bagel. The kitchen told her breakfast would arrive in twenty minutes, so she headed for the shower. As she stood beneath the warm water and let it pour over her head, she wondered why Thomas romping around like a goat should bother her so much. She figured maybe it was because she expected more from him, at the very least to have better taste in women. True, Holly was still beautiful, and it had been ten years since high school. Maybe Holly had changed and become a nice person, but Brina doubted it.

She reached for her shampoo and worked the lather through her hair. Maybe Brina had built Thomas up in her mind to be something he wasn't. She'd used the

evolved: sich … weiterentwickelt
pool: Gruppe
punch: schlagen • 3:00 A.M.: 3 Uhr morgens • exhausted: erschöpft
dialled: wählte • bagel: (weiches, ringförmiges Brötchen) • headed for: machte sich auf den Weg zur • romping around like a goat: der wie eine Ziege herumtollte • bother: ausmachen • at the very least: zumindest
worked the lather through her hair: massierte den Schaum ins Haar ein • built … up: hochstilisiert

blueprint of the boy she'd known, the boy who'd gone to movies with her just so she wouldn't have to go alone, to create someone who was perhaps larger than life. But people changed. Thomas had changed. He'd become … a man.

After her shower, Brina wrapped her hair in a towel and brushed her teeth. A loud knock shook her door and she quickly stepped into a pair of beige lace panties. She grabbed her white silk robe and called out, "Just a minute," as she slid her arms into the sleeves. She pulled ten dollars out of her wallet and hurried to tie the belt about her waist. At nine in the morning, she figured room service was used to seeing people in their bathrobes. But when she opened the door, it wasn't room service. Thomas stood on the other side, looking fresh and clean and very rested for a man who'd spent the night trying out the sexual positions of animals with the prom queen. His white T-neck was tucked inside a pair of black ski pants, and the word DYNASTAR was printed up each of his long sleeves.

"I thought you'd be up," he said.

Brina looked down at herself and pulled the robe tighter around her waist and breasts. "I wish you'd called."

"Why?"

She looked up into his blue eyes and stated the obvious. "I'm not dressed, Thomas."

"I've seen you naked before."

"When?"

"When your swimsuit bottoms came off."

"I was eight. We've both grown a bit since then."

"You're still short."

Room service arrived, and before she knew what he was doing or could protest, Thomas paid the waiter, then carried the tray inside. Brina shut the door behind him as his long strides took him across the room. He set the tray on the table in front of the windows, then flipped the heavy drapery aside to find the

Entwurf • überlebensgroß • Handtuch • Spitzenhöschen • Seide • Morgenmantel • sie ging davon aus • Rolli • (Marke für Skiartikel) • Bikinihöschen • Schritte • schob den schweren Vorhang beiseite

pull string. The curtains folded back and the bright morning light poured into the room, reaching all the corners except the small entry where Brina stood.

Zugschnur • Vorhänge

She leaned back against the closed door and studied his short dark hair cut straight across the back of his tan neck. Her gaze took in the width of his shoulders and back, his narrow waist and nicely rounded buns. His legs had always been long, his feet big, and suddenly the room felt a whole lot smaller. The clean fresh scent of his skin mingled with the smell of coffee, and Brina's stomach twisted into a hungry little knot. She didn't know which was most responsible for the hunger pain. The sight of her bagel or the sight of Thomas.

gebräunt • Pobacken

vermischte sich

Then he turned and looked at her, and she knew. His face was more devastatingly handsome, the symmetry a bit more perfect, in the natural light of day. His skin seemed more smooth and a shade more tan. He looked more … The word that came to mind was *swarthy*. The mixture of his Anglo father's and Spanish mother's blood created a powerful illusion of passion and control.

eine Schattierung • dunkelhäutig • angelsächsisch • Leidenschaft

She felt naked in front of him and pulled the towel from her head. Her damp hair fell past her shoulders

feucht

Setzen Sie die Wörter in Klammern richtig zusammen.

Übung 15

1. Brina woke the next morning feeling ____________ (retid).
2. She had ended up at Mark's ____________ (esouh) with a ____________ (hcubn) of his friends.
3. His friends had not ____________ (voveled) that much.
4. Brina had been ____________ (kawea) all night.
5. She had become so ____________ (gryan) at Thomas that she would have liked to ____________ (puhcn) him.
6. At eight-thirty in the morning she was ____________ (uxsheated).
7. She ____________ (laidlde) room service.

and covered her breasts and back. "Why aren't you out skiing with Holly?"

goss … ein

Instead of answering, he poured a cup of coffee. "Did you leave with Mark last night?" he asked as he blew into the cup and took a drink.

"I went to his party, but it was boring, so I left."

wie bedauerlich • unaufrichtig

He lowered the cup and raised a dark brow. "That's a shame," he said, sounding very insincere as he walked toward her, his long strides silently closing the distance between them. He seemed more relaxed this morning. More like the easygoing boy she'd grown up with, and less like the man she'd met the night before.

unkompliziert

augenscheinlich • elektrisierten • Elektroschocker • Schein

In contrast to Thomas's apparent ease, Brina's nerves zapped her like the Stun Master she sometimes carried for work. She took the cup from him and held out the ten-dollar bill in her hand. "Take this."

"Keep your money, Brina."

steckte es • Hosentasche • Schichten • glatt • riss • verstopft

Instead of arguing, she leaned forward and shoved it deep inside the hip pocket of his ski pants. The second her hand slid between the thin layers of slick nylon and Gore-Tex, she realized it was a mistake. Thomas froze and she jerked her hand free, but it was too late. The air between them changed, becoming clogged

Übung 16

Ordnen Sie die folgenden Begriffe den passenden Wortfeldern zu: **buns, curtains, swimsuit, elevator, teeth, towel, fingertip, panties, waist, shower, belt, elbow, chandelier, throat, tray, sleeves, toe, pants, room service, robe, pocket**

body parts: ______________________________

____

____

dress: ______________________________

____

____

with tension. She placed her hand behind her back, the heat from his body still warming her fingertips. She was pretty sure he'd dressed left, and she didn't know if she should apologize or pretend she didn't know. She decided on the latter but couldn't quite meet his gaze. She stared at his chest and asked, as if she weren't dying of embarrassment, "Did you come here to pour me coffee?"

Anspannung • dass er Linksträger war • sich entschuldigen • so tun als • ihm … in die Augen schauen • Verlegenheit

"I want you to ski with me."

She looked up into his face and was relieved when he stared back as if nothing had happened. "I told you I don't know how to ski."

erleichtert

"I know. I'll teach you."

"I don't even have a ski jacket."

"You can rent what you need." She was about to argue that she didn't need anything because she didn't want to ski when he added, "I'll pay for everything."

leihen • argumentieren

"No, you won't."

"Fine, I won't." He glanced at his silver wristwatch. "The rental shop opened five minutes ago."

"You called?"

"Of course. How long will it take you to get ready?"

Brina considered her options. She could let Thomas teach her to ski, or she could sit in the lodge and hope

hotel: ______________________________

____

____

____

Übung 17

Bitte übersetzen Sie die folgenden Wendungen:

1. to catch up on the past: ______________________

2. to head for the door: ______________________

3. to hang out at a bar: ______________________

she found someone to talk to for the next five or so hours. "Thirty minutes."

Thomas ran his gaze over Brina, a quick sweep up and down of his eyes. He took in her silk robe and damp hair, her flawless skin and pink toe polish. "Can you make it twenty? The rental shop runs out of small sizes early." He reached past her and grasped the door handle. "I'll meet you in the lobby," he said, and walked out of the room and into the hall. The scent of her shampoo followed him, filling the air with the fragrance of coconuts and kiwis.

Schwingen • Nagellack • Duft

He walked to the end of the hall and let himself into his suite. The far wall consisted mostly of windows and overlooked the ski runs below, and the curtains were pulled back to allow the golden sunlight to spill into the room. The light caught in cut-crystal glasses in the bar, and shot multicolored prisms across the thick beige carpet.

bestand ... aus • überblickte • Kristallgläser • Prismen

His skis leaned against the stone fireplace. His Hugo Boss suit he'd worn the night before was flung across the arm of an overstuffed couch, and the napkin with Holly's telephone number had fallen from his pants pocket and lay on the mahogany coffee table.

achtlos ... geworfen • zu prall gepolsterten • Papierserviette

Übung 18

Bitte füllen Sie die Lücken, sodass sich Wörter aus der Geschichte ergeben.

1. A profession: me__ __a__ic
2. A fabric: sil__
3. A game for two players only: c__e__s
4. A kind of nut: co__ __nut
5. A musical instrument: g__i__a__
6. An emotion: em__ar__a__s__ent
7. A toy: __o__l
8. An eye color: h__ __el
9. A weapon: s__e__r

Despite what he'd told Brina, he hadn't considered Holly's invitation. Well, maybe, he'd *considered* it, but not for more than a few minutes. Holly Buchanan was as gorgeous as ever, but he didn't suffer under the delusion that it was his personality alone that turned her on. And frankly, he liked to do the pursuing.

He walked into the bedroom, took his black ski boots out of the closet, and shoved his feet inside. The woman he felt like pursuing at the moment was just down the hall. Last night, when she'd walked up to him and asked him to dance with her, he hadn't been sure he wanted to trip down memory lane with Brina McConnell.

Then he'd taken Brina into his arms, and the longer he'd held her there, the more he'd become convinced that he was going about the whole Brina situation wrong. He decided to discover why she'd fascinated and consumed his teenage years. Growing up, she hadn't even been all that cute. Not until junior high school anyway, and not like now.

Thomas finished buckling his boots and stood. Since he was in town until the next afternoon and had no real plans, he figured he owed it to himself to figure it out before he left. There was a part of him that thought maybe she owed him too, owed him for all the times he'd kept his hands to himself when what he'd really wanted was to run them all over her body. When he'd wanted to taste more than her lips and her throat, when he'd wanted to put his mouth on her breasts and run his hands up her soft thighs.

If he were completely honest, he'd admit that part of his plan had little to do with the girl from the past and everything to do with the woman who'd opened the door wearing her hair in a towel, cheeks pink from her shower, and her nipples marking the front of her white silk robe. He was far more attracted to the woman who'd blushed when she'd shoved money in his ski pants and found more than she'd bargained for than

trotz

umwerfend • litt • Täuschung • die sie anmachte • Jagen

in Erinnerungen schwelgen

falsch anging

beherrscht • niedlich • Mittelschule • festzuschnallen

schuldete • es herauszufinden

Oberschenkel

Brustwarzen

errötet • erwartet

to Holly, who'd shoved her phone number in his pocket while telling him exactly what she wanted.

Remembering Brina's face at the exact moment she'd realized where she'd put her hand brought a smile to Thomas's lips. He chuckled as he pulled his ski poles from the corner he'd leaned them in yesterday. If she wasn't careful, the next time she touched him would be no accident.

lachte in sich hinein • Skistöcke • Zufall

The last day of the year 2000 turned out to be spectacular. The sun shined from an almost cloudless sky, and the temperature hovered around thirty degrees. Perfect skiing weather.

hielt sich um den Gefrierpunkt (30° F = ca. -1° C)

"Are you sure I'm not going to fall off?"

"Yes, and if you do, I'll catch you."

Even though Thomas seemed to know what he was doing, Brina was a bit uneasy. Sure, he'd helped her rent the right clothing and gear, the right length of poles and skis, but she wasn't so sure about the chairlift.

Ausrüstung

The lift line moved forward and Brina planted her poles and moved with it. They'd only run through a few quick lessons before moving into the lift line.

"Shouldn't we try the bunny hill first?"

"Bunny hill's for weenies. You don't want to be a weenie."

Lift-Schlange • steckte … in den Schnee • Idiotenhügel • Weicheier

Actually, she could live with that. "In this outfit, I'd fit right in," she said, referring to the dorky one-piece suit that zipped up the front and cinched in at the waist. It was powder blue with the brand name Patagonia embroidered on her left breast.

"You look cute," Thomas said, trying to sound sincere, but his smile was just a little too amused. In contrast to Brina, Thomas didn't look like a dork. Dressed completely in black, he looked like one of those pro skiers photographed in a Ray-Ban ad.

und bezog sich • dämlich • einen Reißverschluss hatte • auf Taille gearbeitet war • gestickt • aufrichtig • Idiot • Profi- • Reklame

"Well, I can't stop thinking about the last time I went skiing. I can't stop thinking about falling and breaking my leg again, only this time when those really cute ski patrol guys come for me, I'm wearing an Easter Bunny suit. She scratched her nose with her gloved hand. "I'm thinking about how much that will suck." Thomas looked at her through sunglasses so dark she couldn't even begin to see his eyes. "Then don't think about it."

She frowned. "Gee, wished I'd thought of that." They moved forward in line, and she ran through the instructions he'd given her on how to get on the chair-lift. Look back, grab the bar on the outside of the chair with her outside hand, and sit when the chair hit the back of her thighs. Easy.

To her surprise and relief, and with Thomas's help, getting on the lift was easier than she'd thought. Staying on was harder. Her boots and skis were so heavy she felt as if they would pull her off. Her slick suit didn't help.

She panicked and grabbed the back of the chair. "I'm sliding off."

Thomas reached above their heads and lowered the safety bar. Brina rested her skis on the bottom peg and relaxed as the chair lifted them up and up, high above the snowcapped trees. The people below resem-

Pistenrettung • Osterhase • die im Handschuh steckte • wie ätzend das sein wird • na toll • ging die Anleitung durch • Stange • gegen … schlug

draufzubleiben

rutsche ab • Sicherheitsbügel • Fußstütze • schneebedeckt • wirkten wie

Übung 19

Bitte setzen Sie die korrekten Präpositionen in die Lücken ein.
across, against, at, from, into, into, of, out, out

1. Brina moved her palm ____________ his shoulder.
2. She might hang ____________ at the lodge.
3. Thomas blew ____________ the cup of hot coffee.
4. The heat ________ his body was still warming her fingertips.
5. She was dying ____________ embarrassment.
6. He glanced ____________ his wristwatch.
7. He walked ____________ of the room and ____________ the hall.
8. His skis leaned ____________ the fireplace.

bled brightly colored ants, and only the sound of the cable running between the lift wheels filled the crisp air that brushed her cheeks.

Ameisen • kalt

"What kind of private investigating do you do?" Thomas asked, breaking the silence.

She looked over at him, his dark hair and black coat in stark contrast to the backdrop of clear blue sky. His cheeks were beginning to turn pink, and the bright sun shot sparks like solar flares off the dark reflective lenses of his shades. Her pupils contracted and she lowered her gaze to his full lower lip. "Missing persons mostly," she answered. "Sometimes I investigate insurance fraud."

krass • Hintergrund • Funken • Sonneneruptionen • Sonnenbrille • verengten sich

His mouth formed the word, "How?"

"Investigate fraud? Well, say an insurance company based back east somewhere needs some work done in Portland. They call my office and hire me to research a claimant's charge. For instance, last year a woman fell at the place of work and supposedly hurt her back and was confined to a wheelchair. She filed a workmen's compensation claim, but nobody had seen her fall and there were no security cameras. The insurance company hired me and I followed her around for about three weeks."

mit Sitz im Osten • beauftragen • Forderung eines Antragstellers • angeblich • an den Rollstuhl gefesselt • Schadensersatz für einen Arbeitsunfall

Übung 20 Bitte übersetzen Sie die folgenden Sätze ins Deutsche.

1. The people below resembled colorful ants. ____________

2. The sound of the cable filled the crisp air. ____________

3. His cheeks were beginning to turn pink. ____________

4. Her pupils contracted and she lowered her gaze. ____________

5. Brina followed the woman around for about three weeks. ____________

"Isn't that dangerous?"
"Boring mostly. But I finally photographed her driving bumper cars with her kids in Seaside." — Boxauto
"You always were a tenacious little thing." He smiled, a flash of white teeth against his tan lips. "I thought you were going to be a nurse." — hartnäckig • Krankenschwester
Watching his mouth did funny things to her stomach, and she wondered what it would be like to kiss him. To lean over and press her cool lips to his, kiss him until the temperature changed and their mouths turned hot and moist. She turned her gaze and looked down at the tree tops. "And you were going to be a doctor."
His quiet laughter drew her attention to his mouth once again. "You used to give me 'medicine powder' you'd made from crushed Smarties."
"And you used to give me shots in my bottom." — Spritzen • Hintern
"But you never pulled your pants down very far. All I ever saw was the top of one cheek."
"Is that why you wanted to give me shots all the time? You wanted to see my bum?"
"Oh yeah."
"We were in grade school!" — Grundschule
He shrugged. "I don't have any sisters, and after your swimsuit fell off that one time, I was curious." — neugierig

6. She photographed the claimant driving bumper cars with her kids. ______________________

____

7. Brina turned her gaze and looked down at the tree tops. ____

____

8. She wondered what it would be like to kiss him. __________

____

9. Brina used to give Thomas 'medicine powder' she had made from crushed Smarties. ______________________

____

____

Perverser

"You were a little pervert."

A cloud passed across the sun, and from behind the dark lenses of his glasses, she felt his gaze on her, looking as if he could see beneath the blue ski suit. "You have no idea," he said, and something hot and liquid curled in her belly. Thomas Mack had wanted to see her bum. He hadn't been the harmless little friend she'd always thought. Not quite the innocent boy whom she'd helped build a tree fort near the old forest service road not far from his house.

flüssig • kräuselte sich • unschuldig • Baumfestung • Forstverwaltung • näherte sich

The chair lowered and approached the top of the lift. Thomas raised the safety bar. "Do you remember how I told you to get off the chair?"

She transferred her poles to her inside hand.

Schneepflug

"The most important thing is to make a wedge like we practiced at the bottom of the hill."

She nodded as her skis slid along the snow and she stood. The edge of the chair pushed her forward and for a few brief moments she thought, I'm doing good. Then the ramp dipped and curved to the left. Brina continued straight forward and picked up speed.

Rand • kurz • Rampe • neigte sich • schwenkte nach • wurde schneller • richte … aus

"Point your skis in the direction you want to go," Thomas yelled from somewhere behind her.

Übung 21 Welcher der beiden Begriffe ist jeweils der richtige?

1. The sky was almost ____________ (cloudless / cloudlessly) and Thomas was dressed __________________ (complete / completely) in black.
2. Getting on the ski lift was _________________ (more easy / easier / easiest) than she had thought.
3. They had not seen each other _____ (for / since) ten years.
4. Brina was no longer as skinny ____________ (as / than) she had been ____________ (while / during) her high school years.

"What?" She frantically dug her poles into the snow to stop, but it was no use. She slid straight off the ramp and into orange plastic netting that had been strung up like a fence to keep skiers out of the trees. The tips of her skis poked through the holes in the orange plastic as she grappled with it. She didn't fall, but only because she'd grabbed the top of the fencing and held tight.

"Brina."

She looked over her shoulder.

"Are you okay?"

A little girl no taller than Brina's waist swished past on a pair of tiny skis and shook her head as if to say, "What a doofus."

"How do I get out of this?"

Thomas moved behind her, grabbed ahold of her belt, and pulled her free. He moved on the downhill side and informed her of the new plan. "Hold on to my pole and I'll ski in front of you. Use your wedge and I'll steer."

Brina had her doubts, but the new plan worked pretty well. On the slight incline of the cat track, he controlled their speed, his skis perfectly together, the tails moving effortlessly from side to side, making an elongated pattern like a snake in the snow. She held her poles in one hand, the basket of his in the other, and instead of watching the pines or other skiers who passed, she studied the backs of Thomas's powerful thighs. He made it look so easy.

They stopped at a trail marker, their skis horizontal, and Brina looked down the mountain.

"I thought we were going to ski down a beginner run."

"This is."

She wrapped her arm around his to keep from sliding. Beneath the layer of his coat, his muscles felt rock-hard. "It looks like Mount Everest."

He glanced down at her. "Are you scared?"

voller Panik • geradewegs • Netz • aufgehängt • Zaun • stachen • kämpfte

sauste

Doofi

steuere

leicht • Neigung • blau markierten Piste • Enden • mühelos • länglich • Teller (seines Skistocks) • Kiefern • Hangmarkierung • Anfängerhügel

um nicht abzurutschen • steinhart

"I don't want to break my leg again."

"Let's try this," he said as he removed her arm from his. He slid her in front of him and transferred his poles to one hand. "I saw this at a ski school for little kids." He came up behind her, his skis on the outsides of hers, the tips pointed inward. He pressed his palm into her stomach and pulled her back against his chest. The insides of his thighs brushed the outsides of hers, and the top of her head fit just beneath his chin.

Brina looked up at him, her mouth a few inches from his. The scent of musky shave cream and of crisp mountain air and of him clung to his skin. Their breaths mingled and hung in the air and got trapped in the top of her lungs. If he lowered his mouth just a little, their lips would touch. She wanted them to touch. She wanted to rip off her glove and lay her warm palm against his cool cheek. She felt the heat of him through their nylon and Gore-Tex ski pants. Impossible, yet through all those layers he warmed her back and behind, her thighs and low in her abdomen. "What do you want me to do?" she asked her reflection in his glasses.

"Put your poles together and hold them about halfway down, straight out in front of you like you're a waiter."

"Why?"

"Don't really know." He shook his head and his chin brushed her temple. "I saw an instructor make a class of little kids do it. I think it might have something to do with balance. But I want you to do it so you don't stab me in the leg."

She laughed and did as he asked. "Anything else?"

"Let me do the driving. And relax," he added, just above her ear. Then he turned their skis and they slid down the mountain and made elongated Cs.

Relax. She tried, and if it hadn't been for his pelvis pressing into hers as he pushed out the tail of his ski to slow them down, or thighs pressing inward to speed

slid – schob
tips • inward – Spitzen • nach innen
fit • chin – passte • Kinn
musky • clung • got trapped – moschusartig • hing • blieb hängen
rip off – wegreißen
behind • abdomen • reflection – Hintern • Unterleib • Spiegelbild
halfway – halb
waiter – Kellner
stab – stichst
pelvis – Becken
speed – beschleunigen

up, relaxing might have been possible. She might have actually relaxed enough to enjoy the wind in her hair and the cool breeze on her cheeks, or the knowledge that she was actually skiing. But she was much too aware of the subtle pressure of his groin against the small of her back. She dropped her hands and pressed her ski poles into her hips.

tatsächlich • Brise

sich … bewusst • subtil

"Are you okay?" he asked over the sound of their skis sliding across snow.

"Yeah." But she wasn't so sure. As Thomas pushed out the tails of his skis, preparing for a turn, he instructed her on the use of her edges. Instead of paying attention, she was thinking about that morning when she'd stuck her hand in his pocket, and she recalled the heat of his semierect penis against her fingertips. Beneath her clothing, her breasts tightened, and the abrasion of her sheer bra against the nylon suit irritated her sensitive skin. He calmly continued to instruct her while she continued to picture him naked. She felt guilty and perverted, and suddenly, she was no longer as afraid of falling down as she was afraid of falling for Thomas Mack.

Kanten • aufzupassen • erinnerte sich • halb erigiert • strafften sich • Reibung • hauchdünn • BH • sich … vorzustellen • schuldig • sich … zu verlieben

He spread his fingers across the front of her suit and spoke next to her ear. "Your hair smells like a piña

• spreizte

Übung 22

Bitte setzen Sie die folgenden Wörter an der richtigen Stelle ein, um die Sätze zu vervollständigen:
backdrop, balance, degrees, snake, shot, zip

1. A long reptile without any feet is called a ______________.
2. A ______________ is medicine given with a needle.
3. The landscape or sky behind an object is called the ______________.
4. You need to keep your ______________ so you won't fall.
5. Thirty ______________ Fahrenheit is freezing cold.
6. Sports jackets often close with a ______________.

colada. In high school you smelled like baby shampoo."

The warmth of his words slid down the side of Brina's neck and the tips of her skis crossed. The heels of her boots lifted, and she pitched forward.

Thomas made a grab for her belt. "Damn," he swore as they both went down in a tangle of arms and legs, skis and poles. He landed on top of her, the air whooshed from her lungs, and they slid about ten feet before skidding to a stop halfway down the mountain.

"Brina?"

She lifted her face from the snow. "Yeah?"

"Are you hurt?" he asked as she felt his weight lifted from her.

She'd lost her poles and skis somewhere, and she turned onto her back. He hovered just above her, and her elbow bumped his chest. He'd planted his hand in the snow by her shoulders, and his thighs straddled her hips. He'd lost one of his skis and the remaining one crossed over the toes of her boots. He'd shoved his sunglasses to the top of his head.

"I'm okay," she answered. "I just got the wind knocked out of me a little bit."

kreuzten sich • fiel • packte • fluchte • Knäuel • zischte • schlitterten • Gewicht • schwebte dicht über ihr • er saß mit seinen Schenkeln rittlings • der übrige • es hat mir nur … den Atem verschlagen

Übung 23 Lösen Sie das Kreuzworträtsel.

Across:

1. negative emotion when you get less than you expected
2. truly
3. a stand which artists use to place pictures on
4. to call out loudly

Down:

5. private road leading to a house
6. musical instrument
7. sensitive area on the side of your head by your eye

He smiled and creases appeared in the corners of his blue eyes. "That was a pretty good header."
"Thanks. Are you hurt?"
"If I am, will you kiss it and make it better?"
"Depends."
"On what?"
"What I have to kiss."
His quiet laughter touched her face. "Forehead," he said.
Brina placed her gloved hands on his cheeks and kissed him between the brows. "Better?"
He looked into her eyes and his lips brushed hers as he nodded. "Much."
Brina's breath got stuck in her chest, her mouth parted, and she waited for his kiss. Instead he pushed himself to his knees and glanced at the three teenaged girls who skied past. "You're lucky," he said, dug the toe of his boot into snow, and stood.
Crisp air and disappointment cooled the hot anticipation spiking her blood pressure. He'd been about to kiss her. Hadn't he? "I know," she said, hoping he mistook the confusion in her voice. "I could have broken my leg again." She sat and looked for her skis.

Fältchen • Köpfer

Kommt drauf an.

Stirn

blieb … stecken • öffnete sich

du hast Glück • grub • Enttäuschung • Erwartung • die ihren Blutdruck antrieb • falsch verstehen würde • Verwirrung

"That isn't what I meant." He lowered his sunglasses onto the bridge of his nose and covered his eyes. "I'll get your gear."

While Thomas rounded up their gear, Brina dug snow out of the wrists of her glove and wondered what he had meant – exactly. The more time she spent with him, the more confused she became. He helped her with her skis and poles, and when they were ready, he skied beside her this time. He told her when she needed to start her turns, and when they reached the bottom of the mountain, she'd only fallen twice more.

As they waited in line at the chairlift, Thomas gave her instructions on how to better use her edges, and he entertained her with a story about the time he hit a "death cookie" and rolled "ass over elbows" down the side of a mountain. They eased into comfortable conversation, the kind shared by two people who'd known each other well, but who'd changed. They'd grown in different directions but were still connected, deep down where visceral memories were kept like wonderful gifts just waiting to be reopened. Brina listened to the sound of his voice and deep laughter and thought she could probably listen to him forever. For the first

Nasenrücken • bedeckte • zusammentrug

Kurven

unterhielt • (großen Brocken aus hartem Schnee) • Hals über Kopf • glitten • verbunden • instinktiv • Geschenke

Übung 24 Bitte bilden Sie jeweils die fehlende Pluralform.

1. foot ______
2. tooth ______
3. wrist ______
4. baby ______
5. woman ______
6. kiss ______
7. wristwatch ______
8. boot ______
9. half ______
10. tray ______

time since he'd walked into her hotel room that morning, she relaxed completely.

Until Holly Buchanan raced up to them like an Olympic downhill skier and sent up a cloud of snow when she stopped. Holly's skintight stretch one-piece hugged her Barbie-doll curves. The suit was the same color as Brina's, and they both resembled bunnies. Only Holly looked like the kind that got to hang out with Hugh Hefner, while Brina looked like she should be delivering dyed eggs.

"I thought you were going to meet us on the back side." Holly spoke to Thomas without sparing Brina a glance. Ten years had passed, but some things hadn't changed. Brina had a life she loved and a career she enjoyed. She was happy and successful, but standing next to Holly still made her feel insignificant.

"I'm teaching Brina to ski."

Finally, from behind the lenses of Holly's blue goggles, she turned her attention to Brina, and Brina felt like she was back in the seventh grade. Perfect Holly Buchanan was looking at her and finding absolutely nothing worth her time. And like in seventh grade, she almost expected Holly to look down her nose and ask Brina if she bought all her clothes at Sears.

"Mark told me you'd changed," Holly said, then turned her attention back to Thomas. "You should come. Everyone is over there. Someone set up gates and we're slalom racing."

"Maybe later," Thomas told her as he and Brina moved forward in the lift line. Holly moved with them.

"Oh, okay." When she gazed at Brina again, it was like she was finally looking at her and seeing something unexpected. A threat. "It's a lot of fun. You should come too."

Brina shook her head. "I don't think so."

She and Thomas moved in position to grab the next chair. She transferred her poles to her inside hand and looked over her outside shoulder. The chair scooped

raste • Abfahrt • hauteng • Einteiler

(Erfinder des „Playboy") • gefärbt • zu schenken

Skibrille

Lohnenswertes • dass … auf sie herabsehen würde • (Versandhaus) • Tore

unerwartet • Bedrohung

hob … hoch

her and Thomas up and lifted them off the ground, leaving Holly behind.

vielleicht ein • Bestätigung

"Wow, that was some outfit," Brina said as Thomas lowered the safety bar. She wanted reassurance. She wanted him to tell her Holly was a horrible person. She wanted him to lie and say she was fat and ugly.

log

zahlt sich aus

"Yeah, all that yoga pays off."

Schlaufen

Irrational anger pushed Brina's brows together and she shoved her hand through her pole straps. "You don't have to ski with me anymore. You can ski with her if you want."

"I know I can."

schlecht im Bett war • irre

She turned her face away and studied a passing pine. She wanted him to tell her Holly was a lousy lay. "So did she really get all freaky like a goat?" When he didn't answer, she looked at him. He gazed straight ahead like she hadn't asked him a question. "What's the matter? Are you embarrassed?"

Ist es dir peinlich?

"Why would I be embarrassed?"

"Because you had some sort of freaky sex with Holly Buchanan. I'd be embarrassed if I were you."

prüder Mensch

"Why? Are you a prude?"

"No."

"Have you ever had freaky sex?"

öffentliche Toilette

She wasn't sure. One time she'd done it in a public rest room with an old boyfriend. "Of course."

He finally looked at her, but he had his sunglasses on and she couldn't see his eyes. "How freaky?"

She didn't want to tell him.

"That's what I thought. You're a prude."

"I am not."

Over the top of his sunglasses, one dark brow lifted up his forehead.

Verstärkung

"I'm not!" she insisted. "I can get freaky." For emphasis she added, "Extremely freaky."

His other brow lifted. "Tell me."

"No."

"If you do, I'll tell you what you want to hear about Holly."

"Bathroom stall at the Rose Garden." She didn't mention that her boyfriend had worked there, the Trail Blazers had been on the road, and the stadium had been virtually empty. "Twice, now it's your turn."

He waited a few moments before he asked, "Do you want all the juicy details about Holly and me?"

She wasn't so sure she wanted to know anything anymore, but she'd come too far to back down. "No. I just want to know what the goat position is."

"I don't know. I didn't have sex with her."

"What?"

"That's what you *really* wanted to hear, isn't it? That I didn't have sex with the girl who used to torment you."

That was exactly what she wanted to hear. "Are you serious? You didn't spend the night with her?"

"No."

"Why did you tell me you did?"

"I didn't, you just assumed."

But he purposely let her assume the worst. Why, she didn't know. There was a lot about the grown-up Thomas she didn't know. Basic stuff. "Where do you live?" she asked him.

Klokabine • (Sportarena in Portland) • (Basketballteam) • auf Tour • praktisch • schlüpfrig • um einen Rückzieher zu machen

quälen

angenommen • absichtlich • das Schlimmste • Grundsätzliches.

Übung 25

Beantworten Sie bitte die folgenden Fragen auf Englisch.

1. How did Brina pay for her ski equipment when she joined the Ski Club? ______________________________

____

2. When did she break her leg?

____

3. How did Mark and his friends play a trick on the Chess Club?

____

____

4. What does Holly wear while skiing? ______________________________

____

He pulled at his gloves. "Not really anywhere at the moment. Several months ago I sold my house in Seattle, and I moved into my condo in Aspen for a while. But unfortunately, I've had to spend a lot of time in Palm Springs with my grandparents."

"Why unfortunately?"

He glanced at her, then away. "My grandfather has health problems," was all he said. "Eventually I'd like to live in Boulder."

"You can just pick up and move wherever you want?"

He shrugged. "I've been unemployed for a while."

"What have you been doing?"

"A little travelling. Some skiing. Watching way too much Sally Jessy."

She wondered what kind of money he'd made that he could afford to take time off to ski and watch talk shows. Mindy had mentioned something about millions, but that could also be an exaggeration like the Kathy Ireland rumor. "What did you do before you became a ski bum?"

"Have you ever heard of BizTech?"

She shook her head. "Sorry."

"Don't be. It's a computer software company I started with two friends about five years ago."

eines Tages • zuckte mit den Achseln • arbeitslos • viel zu viel • (US-Talkshow) • wie viel • verdient • sich leisten • sich freizunehmen • Übertreibung • Skifreak • gründete

Übung 26 Setzen Sie die folgenden Sätze bitte in die Passivform. Beispiel: Tim ate the cake. → The cake was eaten by Tim.

1. Holly wears a skintight ski suit.

____

2. Thomas is teaching Brina how to ski.

____

3. Thomas started a computer software company five years ago.

____

____

4. Holly tormented Brina in high school.

____

Four

Brina listened as Thomas told her about how he'd started his company by selling his Microsoft stock. He told her he created programs to predict business trends, but she had no idea what that actually meant. She didn't care. As they passed over the tops of pines, she just liked sharing the same chair with him and hearing his voice.

Aktien
Es war ihr egal.

They took several more runs before noon, and even though Brina improved each time, she didn't think Picabo Street had anything to worry about. They stopped for lunch, but the restaurants in the lodge were full, so they changed their boots and walked a few blocks to a sub shop.

Mittag • besser wurde • (US-am. Skirennläuferin) • sich Sorgen machen musste • Sandwichbar

After lunch, Brina didn't feel like skiing and pleaded sore ankles. She persuaded Thomas to take her sightseeing around town. They jumped in his Jeep Cherokee with Colorado plates and headed south to the outskirts. They drove past the two-story house where Brina had been raised, then kept driving half a mile to the small home where Thomas had lived. Two kids played with a golden retriever in the front yard, and an old Wagoneer sat parked in the driveway. Seeing it brought back memories of the many times she and Thomas had walked or run into that house, his grandmother calling for them to take their shoes off.

• berief sich auf wehe Knöchel • überredete • Kennzeichen • Stadtrand • zweistöckig

Vorgarten • (Typ Geländewagen) • parkte • Einfahrt

"Do you suppose the carpet is still that sculpted green stuff?"

He glanced at her, then back at the house. "Maybe. It was guaranteed to survive a nuclear holocaust."

"I wonder if our tree fort survived the years."

"I doubt it."

"I bet it has."

Teppich • wie gemeißelt • hätte garantiert einen Atomangriff überstanden • wette

Thomas took off his sunglasses and threw them on the dash. "What do you want to bet?"

Armaturenbrett • Dollar

"Ten bucks*."

"I don't think so." He looked over at her. "If we bet, I get to name my prize."

aussuchen • Preis

"I'm not going to show you my butt."

He laughed. "I wasn't thinking about your butt."

"Then what?"

"I'll let you know when I win."

She was a bit worried about what he would claim if he won, but she figured he wouldn't really make her do something she objected to. "If I win, you have to buy me a bottle of champagne." And since he didn't seem worried in the least, she added, "And you have to drink it from my boot."

einfordern • das sie ablehnte • da • ganz und gar nicht beunruhigt

He chuckled. "I don't think so."

"Okay, but you have to buy me good champagne. No cheap stuff."

A half mile from Thomas's old house, he pulled the Jeep into the entrance of a forest service road. The road was barricaded by a gate, but the dense growth of pine had kept the snow from becoming too deep.

dichte Wuchs

Thomas went over the barricade first, then Brina. As she swung both legs over the top of the gate, she

schwang

info

Ein gängiger umgangssprachlicher Ausdruck für den dollar ist buck oder auch greenback (vermutlich wegen des grünen Hintergrunds der Dollarnoten). 1000 Dollar werden in der Umgangssprache gerne grand (oder einfach nur G) genannt. Bei den Dollarmünzen heißt das Zehncentstück auch dime und das Fünfcentstück nickel.

Bitte beachten Sie, dass – anders als im Deutschen – im Englischen die logische Pluralform für alle Summen, die größer als one dollar, one euro usw. sind, eingehalten wird. Es heißt also ten dollars, fifty euros usw.

looked down at him as he reached for her waist. She placed her gloved hands on his shoulders and he slowly slid her down the front of his slick coat. "You don't weigh much more than you used to," he said, and set her on her feet.

Brina knew better. She'd weighed ninety-five pounds when she'd graduated, and she'd gained at least fifteen pounds in the past ten years.

The perfect white snow covered the tops of their boots and ankles as they walked side by side down the narrow road cut into the side of a mountain. Brina had been sure she'd recognize the area where she'd spent so much time as a child. She didn't.

"Do you know where we're going?"

"Yep." Their shoulders bumped and he asked, "Cold?"

Walking through the snow, she was actually getting a bit hot. "Not at all. Are you?"

"Nope." Thomas looked over her head, searching the area. "Do you have a boyfriend?" he asked as if he didn't care one way or the other. "Are you seeing anyone?"

"No. You?"

"Not at the moment."

She tripped on a rock hidden beneath the snow and grabbed his arm to keep from falling.

He looked across his shoulder at her. "Graceful as ever, I see."

Brina gazed up into his face. It was true. As a kid, she'd never been real coordinated, but then, contrary to how he looked now, Thomas hadn't been born perfect either. She dropped her hands from his arm. Perhaps he needed a reminder, too, "What happened to your unibrow?"

"Same thing that happened to yours." He stopped and pointed off to their right. "I think it's over there."

Totally directionless, Brina followed him across a small meadow. He paused, looked around, then led her through a dense crop of towering pine. Under-

nach … griff • legte

wiegst

zugenommen

erkennen

Nö.

so oder so • Bist du mit jemandem zusammen? •

stolperte

graziös

koordiniert

Gedächtnisstütze • zusammengewachsene Augenbrauen

ziellos • Wiese • Gruppe • hoher • Gestrüpp

knackte • schlenderten • Lichtung

growth crunched beneath their boots as they walked about fifty feet, then the trees cleared and they strolled into a small clearing where the powdery snow reached their ankles once again.

"There it is." Thomas pointed to a pine directly in front of them.

vergammelt • Bodenbretter • Stufen • verfault • die Wette ist unentschieden

Brina moved closer and looked up at the old deteriorated floorboards of their fort. The steps were gone and several of the boards had rotted and fallen to the ground. "Part of it is still there. I guess the bet is a tie."

Thomas moved to stand behind her. "Or we both win half." He laid his hands on her shoulders, then slid them down the slick arms of her ski suit. "I pay for half a bottle of champagne, and I get half of what I want."

Brina turned and looked up into his face. The shade from the tree cast a shadow over his forehead. "Which is?"

kaum lauter als ein Flüstern

He pulled her close and said just above a whisper, "I get half of you."

He was kidding, of course. "Which half?" she asked.

untere Hälfte

"The top." He placed a hand on the back of her head and lowered his face to her. "Or maybe I'll take the bottom half." His warm breath brushed her lips. "I've always wanted a good look at the bottom half."

Brina's breath caught in her throat, right next to her nervous laughter. Maybe he wasn't kidding. "Keep your hands off my bottom."

stumm • strichen • heiße Schauer • Wirbelsäule

He laughed silently against her mouth. "Wanna bet I can get you to change your mind?" He didn't wait for her answer before he kissed her. Slightly parted, his lips swept across her mouth and sent hot shivers down her spine.

stellte sich auf die Zehenspitzen • Zunge

Her hands moved to his shoulders and slid to the back of his neck. She rose onto her toes and leaned into his chest. "I'm so glad I'm here with you," she whispered, then she touched the tip of her tongue to his warm top lip.

Through his thick gloves, his fingers tightened and tangled in her hair. He tilted her head back, her mouth parted even further, but instead of going after a full-blown kiss, he softly sucked her bottom lip. With each slick pull of his hot moist mouth, she felt a responding tug at her breasts and between her legs and in her heart. Her eyes fluttered closed as she let the sensations pour through her like warmed honey, thick and sweet.

verstärkten den Druck • verhedderten sich • richtig • saugte sanft an • Ruck • schlossen sich mit flatternden Lidern • Gefühle • der

This wasn't the boy she'd known. This man melting her in the middle of winter knew what he wanted, knew what he was doing, right down to the teasing command of his mouth. He'd been here before and was very, very good at seducing thoughts out of her head. This Thomas was someone she'd never met. Someone who made her crave more than the touch of him through thick clothes. She pulled off her gloves and dropped them to the ground. Bare now, her fingers combed through the short hair on the sides of his head. Cool and silky, it curled around her knuckles and tickled her palms.

sie zum Schmelzen brachte • neckend • Herrschaft • zu locken

zu begehren

nackt • kämmten • wickelte es sich • Fingerknöchel

Thomas tilted her face to one side and pressed his lips more fully into hers. His mouth opened and closed, then opened again in imitation of a man now hungry

Übung 27

Ordnen Sie bitte die folgenden englischen Wörter den deutschen Übersetzungen zu.

I bet – I guess – I'm kidding – I assume – I feel – I figure – I believe – I think

1. Ich glaube, ich denke (formal) ________________

2. Ich glaube, ich denke (umgangssprachlich) ________________

____

3. Ich wette ________________

4. Ich habe das Gefühl ________________

5. Ich gehe davon aus, ich nehme an (formal) ________________

6. Ich meine es nicht ernst ________________

for something a little more filling. His tongue swept into her mouth for a hot sexual assault, devouring her and creating a tight suction. He kissed her long and hard, their tongues touching, exploring tastes and textures until a groan was dragged from deep within his chest. He pulled back and looked into her face, his breathing harsh as he sucked air into his lungs.

No, this was not the Thomas who'd done little more than hold her hand and kiss her lips. This Thomas stared at her from beneath lowered lids, letting her see exactly what he wanted. He wanted more than her hand, and from somewhere inside, down where all of her memories and old feelings were stored, somewhere near the bottom of her heart, the past and present mixed and converged in a tangle of confused emotions, and the boy she'd loved was quickly becoming a man she could let herself fall in love with.

"Remember all those times I came to your house?" he asked, his voice rough. "Your mom would answer the door, and I'd ask if you could play."

"Mmm-hmm."

He bit the middle finger of each glove and threw them to the ground. "What do you say, Brina?" He reached for the zipper of her ski suit and looked into her eyes.

sättigend • Angriff • verschlingend • Sog • erforschte • Geschmäcker • Konsistenzen • Stöhnen • aufstieg • scharf

Lider

gespeichert

trafen zusammen

rau

Übung 28 Welche der angegebenen Möglichkeiten ist korrekt? Kreuzen Sie sie an. (Es ist nur jeweils eine Lösung möglich.)

1. ☐ Brina has always been in love with Thomas.
☐ Brina is afraid of falling in love with Thomas.
☐ Brina is in love with a man in Portland.

2. ☐ Thomas had sex with Holly last night.
☐ Thomas spent last night talking to Holly about goats.
☐ Thomas ignored Holly's offer to have sex with her.

He didn't ask for permission, but she knew she could stop him if she chose. "Wanna play?"
"What do you have in mind?" she asked, even though she figured she already knew.
"Some of this." Slowly he pulled the zipper down the middle of her chest and lower. Cold air slipped between the metal tracks and hit her heated flesh. Her skin tightened and her nipples puckered to hard, almost painful points. And still he stared into her eyes even as he grasped the edges of the suit and pushed them aside. "Some of that."
Brina held her breath and waited. Several prolonged moments passed until he lowered his gaze past her chin, down her throat to her sheer bra. Suddenly everything within him went still; he blinked twice, then shook his head as if he were taken aback.
"Jesus, you're not wearing a shirt."
"Was I supposed to?"
"I guess not," he said as he slid his hand inside. His warm palm touched her stomach, then slipped upward to cup her. "You might not have had your growing streak until after high school, but it was worth the wait. You're perfect."
Brina's breath hitched in her chest, and she pushed

Erlaubnis • willste

Kanten • Fleisch • spitzten sich

ausgedehnt

in • zwinkerte • überrascht

Sollte ich das? • wohl nicht • um … zu umschließen • das Warten hat sich gelohnt • blieb stecken

3. ☐ Thomas doesn't care how much a bottle of champagne costs.
☐ Thomas cannot afford to buy a bottle of champagne.
☐ Thomas can only afford to buy half a bottle of champagne.

4. ☐ Brina has lost the bet and has to buy a bottle of champagne.
☐ Thomas has lost the bet and has to do whatever Brina wants.
☐ Both have lost half the bet.

5. ☐ Thomas knows how to seduce women.
☐ Thomas doesn't know how to seduce Brina.
☐ Thomas doesn't know how to seduce women.

her breast into his hand as she leaned forward and kissed his jaw. She pulled aside the collar of his coat and shoved down his T-neck. Against the warm flesh of his throat, she pressed her open mouth and tasted him there.

He bent his knees, grabbed the backs of her thighs, and wrapped her legs around his waist. In two long strides, he pinned her back against the tree and brought her face to his. Instantly his mouth on hers was hot and carnal, no sweet kisses this time, no teasing. He pushed the zipper apart and filled his hands. Her nipples grazed the centers of his palms, his fingers squeezed her breasts, and he shoved his tongue into her mouth and his pelvis up against her crotch. Through the Gore-Tex and nylon lining, she felt him long and hard, and she squeezed her thighs around his hips. He braced his feet wide and moved his mouth to her chin and the side of her neck. He kissed the hollow of her throat and the top swells of her breasts. Brina's back arched; she pressed her shoulders into the uneven bark of the tree and combed her fingers through the sides of his thick hair.

The tip of his tongue traced the edge of her bra to the satin bow sewn in the center. Then he slid his closed

beugte
presste
sinnlich
streiften • drückten • Unterleib
er stützte sich breitbeinig ab • Einbuchtung • Wölbungen • bog sich • rau • Rinde • fuhr … entlang • Schleife • aufgenäht

Übung 29 Bitte setzen Sie die Verben in Klammern in die jeweils angegebene Zeitform.

1. Past perfect: She ________________ (to lean) forward.
2. Future I: She ________________ (to taste) his skin.
3. Simple past: He ________________ (to bend) his knees.
4. Going-to future: He ____________________ (to grab) the backs of her thighs.
5. Present tense: She ________________ (to feel) him through the thin material of her suit.
6. Future II: He __________________________ (kiss) the hollow of her throat.

lips across the fullest part of her breast and brushed them back and forth across her puckered flesh. Brina's fingers curled into his hair as he took her nipple into his wet mouth and sucked her through the sheer nylon of her bra.

gekräuselt

A part of her knew she shouldn't allow this, that it was wrong, but it didn't feel wrong. It felt right.

She looked down at his dark head, at the hollow of his cheeks as he drew upon her, and then she closed her eyes and just allowed the feelings he created in her to take control. The feeling of his moist soft tongue through the abrasive material of her bra. The heat slicing through her body and curling the toes inside her boots. She ran her hands through his hair, down his neck and across the shoulders of his coat, then back to his hair, touching him as much as possible, but it wasn't nearly enough. Her hips moved, and through the layers of their clothes, he thrust against her. And it still wasn't enough. She wanted it all. She wanted all of him, but in the end, she was thwarted by their winter clothes.

während er an ihr saugte

reibende • die … schnitt

annähernd • stieß

daran gehindert

Another agonized groan tore from his throat, and he grasped her thighs, stilling her. He lifted his head, and Brina looked into his face, at his wet lips, and the frustration burning bright in his slumberous blue eyes. Cool air replaced the heat of his mouth, finally bringing with it a semblance of sanity and the reality of the situation.

gequält • entfuhr • und brachte sie zur Ruhe • schläfrig

Anschein • Vernunft •

She unlocked her legs from around his hips and slid down the tree until her feet touched the ground. With each passing second, the passion in his eyes cleared until he looked as stunned as Brina felt. She opened her mouth, then closed it again. She didn't know what to say.

löste

entfernte sich • geschockt

Thomas seemed to suffer from the same problem. Without a word, he reached for the tab of her zipper and pulled it up to the base of her throat, sealing the touch of him inside. Then he turned away and

Schiebergriff • und versiegelte so

holte • mitgenommen

retrieved their gloves from the ground. "It's getting late," he finally said. His low voice sounded strained to Brina's ears.

unterzugehen

"Yes," she said, even though they both knew it would be hours before the sun would even begin to set. She took her gloves from him and shoved her hands inside.

belanglos • abdriftete • zogen sich zurück • Knirschen • der die völlige Stille unterbrach

On the walk back to the car, they spoke little. Meaningless conversation really, which lapsed into long periods of silence. Both retreated into their own thoughts, the crunch of snow beneath their boots the only sound disturbing the complete quiet.

Spur

For the first time since Thomas had unzipped her snowsuit, Brina felt her cheeks burn. While he'd had his hands and mouth on her, she hadn't felt one twinge of anything that even resembled embarrassment, but she did now. She wondered what he thought of her. She wondered if he thought she let this sort of thing happen all the time.

sich verlieben

heilig

allzu • verklemmt • verworfen hatte • zugunsten • abliefern • Schmutzwäsche • Zehennägel

Normally she had to fall in love before she let lust take control. Her mother had always taught her that her body was sacred. A temple. There had been several years in college when she'd thought her mother was overly uptight about sexuality and discarded the whole sacred-temple concept in favor of a more modern approach of binge and purge*. She'd binge on a man for a while, then discover something wrong – like he'd drop off his laundry at her apartment, or she'd suddenly notice he had bad toenails – and she'd have to purge.

zurückgekehrt • ziemlich • wählerisch • anbeten • gerne mögen

Now that she was older and wiser, she'd reverted back to her mother's teachings, and was fairly picky about whom she let worship her body. She had to care for the man, and it took time before she felt comfortable enough to let intimacy happen.

Until today.

Auf den Kopf gestellt und verkehrt herum.

Everything was different today. Turned upside down and inside out. Nothing made sense, and she didn't know what to think or how to feel. She wished she did. She wished she had answers for all the questions rolling around in her head. She was a private investigator, and it was her job to search until she found the answers. Only this was her private life and she felt clueless and didn't even know where to begin.

die … kreisten

suchen • hatte keine Ahnung

Thomas helped her back over the barricade, but this time there were no lingering touches. He opened the passenger-side door for her, and she cleared the snow from her boots before she climbed inside. For two people who fifteen minutes before hadn't seemed to have an ounce of restraint or self-consciousness, the awkward silence stretching between them seemed that much more noticeable. The comfortable friendship she'd enjoyed over the past few hours was completely gone.

Unze • Beherrschung • Befangenheit • die sich zwischen ihnen ausbreitete • spürbar

On the drive back to the lodge, Thomas finally broke the silence with, "I think it might snow tonight."

Brina's response was just as inspired. "Oh, uh-huh." She wondered what he was thinking, but his dark glasses once again covered his eyes and concealed even a hint of his thoughts.

Andeutung •

They lapsed back into silence until Thomas pulled the Jeep up to the front doors of the lodge and shoved the

verfielen • den Jeep bis … fuhr

info

To binge bedeutet „sich vollstopfen", während to purge „sich erbrechen" oder „sich reinigen" bedeutet. Binge and purge wird umgangssprachlich für die Krankheit Bulimie verwendet. Rachel Gibson beschreibt damit ironisch Brinas Männerbeziehungen: Erst kann sie nicht genug von einem Mann bekommen – und dann will sie ihn schnell und radikal wieder loswerden.

Übung 30

Bitte bringen Sie die Wörter in die richtige Reihenfolge.

like Brina to men were food for to binge on.

____

____

den Schalthebel auf „Parken“ schob • hören wollte • dass ich die Kontrolle verloren habe • Windschutzscheibe • verriet nichts • ausdruckslos • Gesichtszüge • verschlossen • schade

vehicle into park. When he spoke, it wasn't really what Brina longed to hear. "I'm sorry I got carried away. Normally I don't go around pinning women against trees," he said, as he stared out the windshield.

"Me either. Ah … getting pinned, I mean." She thought a moment. "Maybe it happened because we feel like we know each other."

"But we don't." He finally looked at her, but his face gave nothing away. "We don't know each other at all."

Brina gazed into his expressionless features, and thought he might be right. This closed-up man wasn't the Thomas she'd known. Just when she'd begun to think she knew him, she realized she didn't know him at all. Not anymore. Which, she realized with a heavy heart, was a shame. "Good-bye, Thomas," she said and let herself out of the Jeep.

Drehtüren • legte einen Gang ein • Parklücke • Rückseite • den Motor • was zum Teufel

From behind his sunglasses, Thomas watched Brina walk through the revolving doors of the lodge. He shoved the vehicle into gear and drove to a parking slot on the far side of the hotel. He turned off the engine, leaned his head back against the seat, and closed his eyes.

What in the hell had happened? He couldn't believe

Übung 31 Finden Sie das englische Gegenteil der folgenden Begriffe:

1. to dress ______________
2. poor ______________
3. significant ______________
4. backyard ______________
5. unemployed ______________
6. beautiful ______________
7. skinny ______________
8. top ______________
9. harsh ______________
10. queen ______________

he'd shoved Brina against a tree and buried his face in her breasts. She'd been wrong. It wasn't because he knew her. Ten years ago he'd always been able to stop. It was something else. Something he didn't even like to admit to himself.
He'd lost control. That was what had happened, and he didn't want to think about what he would have done if it were summer and getting Brina out of her clothes was just a matter of flipping up her skirt and slipping off her panties. He was afraid he wouldn't have stopped. He would have made love to her against that tree where they'd played as kids. He would have gladly lost control to Brina McConnell.
What was that saying about being careful of what you wished for? The bet he'd made with her had been a joke. All day he'd pictured her wearing long johns beneath that ski suit, and it had never entered his head that she only wore her bra, and not much of a bra either. Everyone knew you were supposed to wear a base layer. Everyone but Brina, he supposed. When he'd unzipped her suit, he'd thought she would stop him. He'd meant to shock her, but when he'd lowered his gaze, he'd been the one shocked like a kid getting his first look at a centerfold*.

Sie irrte sich. • sich selbst gegenüber zugeben • hochzuheben • Rock • er hätte mit ihr geschlafen • nur zu gern • Spruch • lange Unterhosen • es war ihm nie in den Sinn gekommen • Basisschicht • außer

11. (the) quiet (Substantiv!) ________________
12. to lower ________________
13. divorced ________________

info

Ein centerfold ist die Doppelseite in der Mitte einer Sexzeitschrift, auf der ein nacktes Model in Großaufnahme gezeigt wird.

Now as he sat in his Jeep, he wondered why she hadn't stopped him. Ten years ago she'd always stopped him with that lame "my body is a temple" bullshit excuse her mother had taught her. Now she not only didn't stop him, she squeezed her thighs around him and held his face to her breast, and he couldn't help but wonder why. The easy answer was that they were both adults and enjoyed sex, but Thomas never went for the easy answers. He never would have succeeded in business if he had.

lahm • windige Ausrede

On the drive to the lodge, another thought had entered his head. One he tried to dismiss but failed. He didn't like it, but it was there – a nagging voice in the back of his brain. He'd seen it a lot with the older guys and wimpy geeks he did business with. Beautiful women, women like Holly who were willing to be with anyone, just as long as they had money, and the men kidding themselves that the women wanted them for themselves.

verdrängen • ohne es zu schaffen • nagend • Hirn • erbärmlich • Computerfreaks • bereit • die sich selbst vormachten • ihrer selbst wegen •

Thomas didn't want to believe that Brina could be so shallow, but he hadn't seen or talked to her in ten years. Maybe that was exactly what she wanted. Money she'd never had as a kid and the attention she'd always wanted. To be seen with the biggest fish in the pond.

oberflächlich

Teich

info

Das deutsche Erdgeschoss entspricht in Großbritannien dem ground floor und der erste Stock dem first floor usw. In den USA wird das Erdgeschoss jedoch schon als first floor bezeichnet; der 1. Stock ist demgemäß der second floor usw. Brina und Thomas nahmen also die Treppen hinauf in den zweiten Stock (third floor).

Übung 32

Bitte übersetzen Sie den folgenden Satz ins Englische.

1. Den ganzen Tag lang hatte sich Thomas Brina in langen Unterhosen vorgestellt.

____

____

And even though he knew it probably wasn't fair to judge her by her past, it wasn't as if she hadn't done it before. Only last time he'd been dirt-poor and she'd dumped him faster than yesterday's garbage.

Thomas opened his door and got out of the Jeep. His quick strides carried him into the lodge and past the registration desk. Without waiting for the elevator, he took the stairs to the third floor*. He had to take his mind off her before she drove him completely insane. He had to fill his head with something other than the way she'd grabbed ahold of his insides and twisted him around.

Without pause, he walked past her door and to his own room. He unzipped his coat as he sat on the sofa in front of the fireplace and changed into his ski boots. Even as kids, there'd always been something about Brina. Something that had pulled at him. Something that just crept inside and made him want to wrap his hands in her hair and bury his face in her neck. Last night he'd thought he felt nothing for her, but he'd been wrong. This morning he'd thought he could kiss her and touch her and, maybe, make love to her. Nothing complicated. Just two people who'd known each other as kids, getting together as adults and having a good time. Just a man and a woman wanting to give each other a little pleasure.

He'd been wrong again. They weren't just any man and woman. They were Thomas and Brina, and like some preprogrammed memory, his body responded as if he were seventeen again. Wanting her so much he thought he would die. Only now it was worse.

When he'd held her against that tree and looked into her hazel eyes turning gray with passion, he'd shot past wanting her and had headed straight for need.

Thomas grabbed his skis and walked back out into the hall. The last thing he wanted was to give her that much control. The last thing he wanted was to need Brina McConnell.

beurteilen • bettelarm • den Müll von gestern

Rezeption • nicht mehr an sie denken • verrückt • gepackt • Inneres • umwickelt

etwas Besonderes an • gezerrt • kroch

Spaß • irgendein(e)

vorprogrammiert • reagierte

war er am Wollen vorbeigerast und direkt zum Brauchen übergegangen

Five

Brina squinted through the darkness to the clock next to her bed. It was 10:30 P.M. She'd missed the banquet and the tour of her old school. No big deal, but she'd wanted to hook up with Karen Johnson and Jen Larkin before the awards ceremony. She'd wanted to make sure she had someone to sit with so she didn't look like a complete loner.

spähte • 22:30 Uhr • sich … zusammentun • Preisverleihung • Einzelgängerin

She pushed her hair out of her face and sat on the side of her bed. After Thomas had dumped her at the lodge, she'd changed and gone back down to the lobby. Karen and Jen had been just about to leave to hit all the boutiques in town. Brina had joined them and bought a Galliton sweatshirt to replace the old one she slept in. She'd had a good time talking about the past with girls she had something in common with. Band girls. Home Ec Club girls. The nerds-who-don't-ski girls. She'd helped Karen pick out a little bunting suit for her unborn baby, and they'd stopped for lattes in the old renovated fire station. She'd kept herself occupied, diverted her attention with shopping, and hadn't thought of Thomas very much. Well, not every minute anyway.

wollten gerade • besuchen • sich ihnen angeschlossen • gemeinsam • Hauswirtschafts-AG • Langweiler • Strampelanzug • Milchkaffee • hatte sich … abgelenkt

When she'd returned to the lodge, she'd grabbed the ski equipment she'd rented that morning. There was no use in keeping it since she didn't plan to ski anymore. As she'd stood in line, waiting her turn to return the awful blue suit, laughter had drawn her attention out of the rental shop and into the lounge. Sitting beside a big roaring fire, looking tan and cozy, yucking it up like best friends, were Holly, Mindy Burton, and Thomas.

es war sinnlos • bis sie an der Reihe war • lodernd • behaglich • rissen Witze

While Brina had stood in the rental shop, her stomach

turning, holding the suit Thomas had unzipped and stuck his hands inside, he'd casually flirted with other women.

She'd watched as Thomas leaned forward to hear something Holly had said, and she'd felt a little pinch in her heart and looked away. He'd dropped her off to hang out with Holly and her friends, and that hurt more than she'd thought possible.

After returning the suit, she'd gone to her room and tried to tell herself she didn't care. Her eyes watered anyway, and it was just too bad her heart wasn't listening. She'd turned on the television to watch a little local news before getting ready for the action-packed events planned for that evening. She'd stared up at the ceiling, listening to a report on some stupid city council meeting, and she'd fallen asleep. Unfortunately, she'd had a nightmare involving Thomas and Holly, happy, laughing, together. Now that she was awake, she thought about going back to bed. Seeing Thomas again with Holly just might kill her.

The light from the television flickered and flashed across the room as she tried to imagine what might be happening in the banquet room below. Yes, seeing Thomas with Holly might kill her, but staying in

lässig • Zwicken • sie abgesetzt • tränten • jedenfalls • Zimmerdecke • Stadtratsversammlung • Albtraum • flackerte • blitzte • sich vorzustellen

Übung 33

Bitte setzen Sie die folgenden Wörter in die richtigen Lücken ein.
picky, out, different, upside, wiser, intimate, comfortable

1. Now Brina was older and ______________________.

2. She was fairly ______________________ about whom she let worship her body.

3. She had to feel ______________________ with a man before becoming ______________________ with him.

4. Everything was ______________________ today – turned ________________ down and inside ________________.

sie … fertigmachen • ganz ohne • missverstanden • Begeisterung • schleppte sich • kurzärmelig • Top mit Stehkragen • Sellerie • Fellstiefel • supermodern • veranstaltete • Schlag Mitternacht • föhnte • flocht • locker • Zopf • bestimmt • ringförmige Ohrringe • streute

her room imagining the worst would definitely do her in.

Drained of anything that could be misconstrued as enthusiasm, Brina dragged herself into the shower for the second time that day. When she got out, she dressed in a pair of jeans and a short-sleeved mock T-neck, made of celery-colored stretch satin. The words *Calvin Klein* were written in silver across her breasts. She wore a black leather belt and pulled on her black shearling boots she'd worn earlier. They weren't a great fashion statement, but they would keep her feet warm when she stepped outside to watch the fireworks show the lodge set off every year at the stroke of midnight.

Brina blew-dry her hair, then wove it into a loose braid. She put on cosmetics to make herself feel better, rather than to look good for any particular man. She hung big silver hoops in her ears, wrapped her big silver watch around her wrist, and sprinkled silvery glitter in her hair. She looked short, but she looked good.

Caban (Wolljacke) • gab • hinten zu bleiben • unbemerkt verschwinden • Trophäen • ausgelassen • zu produzieren • Hosenscheißer • den sieben Weltwundern gleichkäme

On the way out, she grabbed the peacoat she'd brought with her from home, and by the time she made it downstairs, it was eleven-thirty. She moved past the ballroom where the reunion had been held the night before. Tonight the lodge was hosting its annual New Year's Eve party, and the reunion had been moved down the hall to a large banquet room.

She walked through the doorway and decided to hang back just in case she wanted to make a quiet exit. Mindy Burton's voice flooded the room from where she stood behind a podium handing out little trophies.

"Our next award goes to the couple with the most children. It goes to Bob and Tamra Henderson. They have seven," Mindy said, in her most cheerful rah-rah voice, as if cranking out seven rug rats in ten years ranked right up there with the seven wonders of the world. Everyone applauded Bob and Tamra's reproductive organs, and Brina began to think that maybe it was just her. Maybe it was her crappy mood, but she deserved a trophy. More like the reunion committee was so lame, they had to think up stupid reasons to give their friends a trophy. Next they would probably give an award for the brownest hair.

Geschlechtsorgane • miese Laune • verdiente • schon eher

She let her gaze skim the crowd, searching for Karen and Jen, but of course, she spotted Thomas first. And of course, he sat at a round table, surrounded by women. As if he felt her gaze on him, he looked up at her, then slowly he rose from his chair. As Mindy announced the next award winner, Brina watched Thomas walk toward her. His face was tanned from the sun, his lips a little chapped. He wore faded Levi's, a white cotton sweater with a navy V-neck, and a plain white T-shirt beneath. With each casual stride of his long legs, her heart raced a bit faster. The faster her heart raced, the angrier she became, and the angrier she became, the more she didn't care if her anger was irrational. He'd kissed her and touched her like she meant something to him, then he'd dumped her and made her feel like she didn't. He made her question his motives and hers. Made her uncertain and unsure. Something she hadn't felt since high school.

über die Menge wandern • umringt

rissig

lässig

Übung 34

Suchen Sie auf dieser Doppelseite Wörter, die in etwa dasselbe bedeuten wie die folgenden Begriffe:

1. sex organ = ______________________

2. misunderstood = ______________________

3. yearly = ______________________

4. silent = ______________________

5. happy = ______________________

6. relaxed = ______________________

7. reason = ______________________

erinnerte sie sich selbst • vertraut • Kloß • Sehnsucht • gebetet • Puppe • am wenigsten • nachließ • sexuell freizügig

He didn't owe her anything, she reminded herself. She didn't owe him anything either. He was a stranger. They were strangers. She didn't know him anymore.

Only he didn't feel like a stranger. When she looked into his familiar blue eyes, she felt as if she were coming home. Her soul recognized his. Thomas was the only person alive with whom she shared certain memories that brought a smile to her lips, a catch to her throat, or a longing to her heart. He was the only one who knew all her childhood insecurities and that in the sixth grade she'd prayed for a Strawberry Shortcake* doll.

"Hey," he said as he stopped in front of her. "You just getting in from somewhere?"

"Yeah, my room."

Mindy announced the award for the person who'd changed the least, and Thomas waited for the applause to die before he spoke. "You've been in your room all night?"

"Yes."

"Alone?"

She knew it. After what had happened that afternoon, he thought she was promiscuous, and of course, she'd also admitted to freaky sex in the Rose Garden, which

Übung 35 Brinas Gefühle sind völlig durcheinandergeraten – genau wie die Ausdrücke in Klammern. Korrigieren Sie bitte die Sätze.

1. Brina is (confused about) Holly dancing with Thomas.
   ____
2. She is (jealous of) falling in love with him. ______________
3. Brina is (uncertain about) her desire to make love to him.
   ____
4. She is (annoyed at) his true feelings. ______________
5. She is (afraid of) the lame committee. ______________

info Lizenzfigur (rothaariges Mädchen mit Hut) von 1977.

didn't help her image. With her peacoat hanging on one arm, she shoved her free hand on her hip. "Where were you all afternoon?"

"With you."

She ignored the flush creeping up her neck. "After you dumped me."

das Erröten

His gaze narrowed a bit. "After we got back to the lodge," he said slowly, "I went skiing."

verengte sich

"Yeah, I saw you *skiing*."

"What is that supposed to mean?"

"Nothing."

"You're mad about something."

sauer

"No, I'm not."

"Yes you are. I could always tell when you were mad. You'd get two little wrinkles between your eyes. You still do."

She'd rather eat worms than tell him why she was mad. She looked past him and searched the crowd until she spotted Karen and Jen. "Excuse me," she said. "I'm going to sit with my friends." She wove her way through the tables, and just as she hung her coat on the back of an empty chair, Mindy announced her next award.

lieber • Würmer

sie bahnte sich ihren Weg

"The award for the person who has changed the most goes to Brina McConnell." Brina looked toward the podium and stilled. She was shocked they'd remembered her. She glanced at Karen and Jen, saw their trophies, and realized everyone got one. Gee, and for a whole split second she'd felt special. She moved to the front of the room and Mindy gave her a cheap trophy cup mounted on an equally cheap hunk of plastic.

meine Güte • Bruchteil einer Sekunde • Pokal • montiert • Brocken

"You look great now, Brina," Mindy told her.

Brina gazed into Mindy's blue eyes and decided not to take offense at that comment. She and Mindy had never been friends, but Mindy had never been purposely mean either. "Thanks," she said. "So do you."

• nicht übel zu nehmen

gemein

She made her way back to the table, and as she sat, she cast a glance toward the doorway. Thomas was no longer standing there, nor was he seated with Holly. She gazed around the room and spotted him talking to George Allen. Thomas had put on his ski coat, and he rested his weight on one leg as he flipped his keys around his index finger. He shook his head, then turned and walked out of the banquet room. Brina couldn't help but wonder where he was going and whom he might be meeting.

"What did you get your award for?" she asked Karen, in an effort to take her mind off Thomas.

"Girl most likely to give birth at the reunion."

"I bet it took them hours to think up that one." She looked at Jen. "What's yours?"

Karen busted up laughing, and Brina hoped it wasn't for something mean, like the girl who'd gained the most weight.

"Most freckles," Jen answered through a frown. "I wanted best hair, but they gave Donny Donovan the award for best hair."

"Isn't he gay?"

"No, his boyfriend is, though."

"Who's his boyfriend?" Brina asked.

"Do you remember a guy who graduated a year ahead of us, Deke Rogers?"

"No," Brina gasped. "Get out! Deke Rogers? The guy who looked like Brad Pitt and raced those muscle cars? Everyone was madly in love with him."

"Yep, everyone including Donny."

She shook her head. "Jeez, why couldn't someone like George Allen do us women all a favor and be gay? No one would care."

"True."

Jen nodded. "Yeah, like no one cares that Richard Simmons is gay, but that Rupert Everett …" She sighed and laid her face in her pudgy hand. "I'd like the chance to turn him straight."

Brina bit her lip to keep from laughing, but Karen had no such qualm. She laughed so loud she drowned out

flipped: schnellen ließ • to give birth: zu entbinden • busted up laughing: brach in Gelächter aus • gasped: keuchte • Get out!: Red keinen Unsinn! • muscle cars: (PS-starke Autos) • including: einschließlich • Jeez: Mensch • Richard Simmons: (US-amerik. Fitness-Guru) • Rupert Everett: (brit. Schauspieler) • pudgy: pummelig • straight: hetero • qualm: Skrupel • she drowned out: dass sie … übertönte

Mindy's voice, and so hard Brina feared she would break her water.

After Mindy handed out the last two awards, she made her final announcement. "Of course, everyone is invited to join the lodge in their celebration to ring in the New Year. Five minutes before midnight, a complimentary glass of champagne will be provided, and I know some of you will be first in line to take advantage of free alcohol."

"Damn right," someone yelled from the back of the room.

"In the morning," Mindy continued, over the drunken laughter of a few classmates who were obviously well past three sheets, "we'll all get together back in the ballroom for our farewell brunch. You won't want to miss this, we have something special planned."

As Brina stood and reached for her coat, she wondered what could possibly outdo cheap trophies.

"Are you two going outside to watch the fireworks?" she asked Karen and Jen.

"Heck no!" they answered in unison.

"Too cold."

"You'll freeze your butt off."

Growing up in Galliton, Brina had always loved to

sie würde ihre Fruchtblase zum Platzen bringen

einzuläuten • gratis • serviert • auszunützen • kostenlos

betrunken • die ... schon viel zu tief ins Glas geschaut hatten

übertreffen

Himmel nein! • einstimmig

Übung 36

Bitte ergänzen Sie die zum jeweiligen Substantiv gehörenden Verben.

Substantiv	**Verb**
1. flood	________
2. worship	________
3. expression	________
4. laughter	________
5. excuse	________
6. gaze	________
7. seat	________
8. invitation	________

watch the fireworks the lodge shot into the sky, but back then, because she hadn't been a guest of the lodge she had to watch from the parking lot. She'd always wanted a front-row seat; she and Thomas had both wondered what the show was like from the other side. Now as she walked down the packed hall toward the ballroom, her gaze searched for him. When each dark-haired man she passed turned out to not be Thomas, her heart sunk a little. She didn't know how she could be so angry at a person, yet at the same time, desperate to see his face.

Parkplatz • in der ersten Reihe

überfüllt • Flur

The ballroom was packed with guests and locals who'd paid to attend. The dress ranged from casual to formal, and the band played mostly moldy oldies. Frank Sinatra and Ed Ames were big favorites. Shafts of fractured light reflected off the mirrored ball and onto the partyers below.

um dabei zu sein • leger • fad • Strahlen • gebrochen • Spiegelkugel • Partygäste • der Kälte trotzen

Since neither Jen nor Karen wanted to brave the cold, Brina made her way around the outside of the room by herself. A hand grabbed her arm from behind and she turned, half expecting to see Thomas.

"Hey, Brina," George Allen said above the music.

Disappointed, she didn't bother with a smile. She didn't want to encourage him. "George."

rang sich kein Lächeln ab • ermutigen

Übung 37 In jedem Satz ist ein Fehler versteckt. Streichen Sie das falsche Wort durch und notieren Sie die richtige Version.

1. All of the guests are inviting to join the celebration.

____

2. The lodge will ring up the New Year.

____

3. Five minutes before midnight a compliment will be provided.

____

4. Any of the guests will be first in line to take advantage of free alcohol. ______________________________

While the band sang something about a lady being a tramp, George made a big show of pulling up his sleeve and looking at his watch. "It's eleven fifty-three," he said. "Seven minutes to midnight."

George had always thought he was a babe magnet, but he'd always been so wrong. "Yeah, you better go get your free champagne."

"That's right." He rocked back on his heels and stared at her through glassy eyes. "I'll be right back. Don't go too far. I plan on giving you a New Year's Eve kiss."

"Oh goody," she told him, but her subtle sarcasm was completely lost on him. "I'll wait right here, I promise."

"Okaaaay," he said, nodding his head, then melting into the crowd.

Brina immediately made a beeline for the deck. She shoved her arms through the sleeves of her coat and pulled her braid from inside. As she buttoned her wool peacoat, she dodged and wove her way through the throng, then she opened the doors and joined the crowd on the deck. The frigid air hit her cheeks and nearly robbed her of breath. She turned up her collar and pulled her thin stretch gloves from her pocket.

Landstreicherin • Frauenheld • er verlagerte das Gewicht auf die Fersen • glasig • super • verschwendet • ging schnurstracks • wich … aus • Gedränge • eisig • nahm ihr fast den Atem • klappte … hoch

5. A few classmates had already drink too much.

____

6. They were obviously well passed three sheets.

____

7. They will get together in the ballroom for there farewell brunch. ______________________________

8. Brina wondered what possibly could outdo cheap trophies.

____

9. She had always loved to watch the fireworks being shot in the sky. ______________________________

10. She had had to watch the parking lot. ____________________

They wouldn't keep her hands warm, but if she shoved them in her pockets, she would be okay.

"Two minutes," the band singer announced over speakers mounted in the corners of the deck. "Grab your champagne and your sweetheart."

Geländer

She made her way to the railing and looked over the side to the people below. Her thoughts once again turned to Thomas. It was really too bad he wasn't around. He'd loved fireworks as much as she had. In fact, he used to make rockets using match heads. Or perhaps he was around, getting ready to watch the show with someone else.

Raketen • Streichholzköpfe

"Brina!"

weiter

She leaned even farther over the rail and waved at Mark. He stood in a group of his friends, Holly included. Brina was a bit surprised that Thomas wasn't with them.

"Come down here," he called up to her. "We have schnapps to keep warm."

Schnaps

The last time she'd drunk schnapps, she'd had a hangover for three days. "No, I'm okay."

Kater

"One minute," the band leader warned.

A bit unsteady on his feet, Mark pleaded, "Pleezze, Brina. Come down or I'll have to come up and get you."

unsicher • bettelte • bitte, bitte

info

Sehr populäres Lied, das in den angelsächsischen Ländern traditionell um Mitternacht an Silvester gesungen wird. Die Melodie ist eine alte schottische Weise; den Text verfasste der schottische Dichter Robert Burns 1788. Wörtlich übersetzt bedeutet der Titel old long since, also in etwa „längst vergangene Zeit". Sie haben die wunderschöne, melancholische Melodie sicher schon einmal gehört!

Übung 38

Alle folgenden sechs Wörter beschreiben Teile der Hand. Setzen Sie bitte zur Vervollständigung die fehlenden Buchstaben ein.

1. n _ _ _	**2.** f _ _ _ _ _	**3.** k _ _ _ _ _ _
4. w _ _ _ _	**5.** t _ _ _ _	**6.** p _ _ _

Brina looked from Mark to Holly, who didn't even bother to hide the fact that she was annoyed as hell about something. "Oh, all right," Brina said, and moved back from the rail. At one time she would have loved to have been invited to stand with those people, and she would have loved the opportunity to annoy Holly even more, but now she just didn't care.

wütend • verdammt

Chance

"Twenty seconds."

She took another step backward and covered her cold ears with her gloved hands. She didn't have any intention of meeting Mark and the others. She wanted to watch from exactly where she stood.

Absicht

The countdown started at fifteen, and around ten, a solid body brushed up against her back and a strong arm reached from behind and wrapped around her stomach. Brina looked over her shoulder, ready to punch George Allen if she needed to. She lowered her hands to her sides and stared up into Thomas's dark face.

"I knew I'd find you out here," he said next to her ear.

She didn't have to ask him how he knew. He, too, remembered all those years they'd stood on the other side, wondering about the view from the deck, and vowing someday to have the money to stand exactly where their feet where now planted.

sich schworen

The countdown continued, three … two … one. From the top of Showboat, the first volley of fireworks shook the ground, the band struck up "Auld Lang Syne*," and Thomas slowly lowered his face and pressed his cool mouth to hers. As bursts of red, white, and gold exploded in the black sky, Brina's chest felt like it exploded too. Her heart expanded thumping wildly against her breastbone, sending blood pounding in her head.

Salve • ließ den Boden erzittern • setzte ein mit • Explosionen

weitete sich • und schlug • Brustbein

Thomas's chapped lips were slightly abrasive, and he tasted of crisp air and smooth scotch. She thought she should probably push him away. She was mad at him and had a right to her anger, but it was quickly

süffig

swallowed up within the onslaught of overwhelming emotion and greed sucking away her will to "just say no." And besides, she rationalized, it was just a New Year's Eve kiss.

geschluckt • Angriff • überwältigend • Gier • die … schwächten

Brina turned in his embrace. With one arm around her back, he pulled her up on her tiptoes, and he placed his cold hand against her equally cold cheek. Their lips parted, and her eyes drifted shut. The frigid night nipped at her face and ears, and inside her mouth Thomas's slick warm tongue touched hers. The kiss continued through "Auld Lang Syne" and several more volleys that Brina felt through the soles of her feet. A hot shiver ran down her spine and her breasts tightened. Neither had a thing to do with the frozen air around her.

Zehenspitzen • genauso • schlossen sich • biss

Thomas misinterpreted her shudder and pulled back. "Are you cold?"

missverstand • Schaudern

Since she didn't want to admit that his kiss left her shaky, she nodded.

zitternd

"I know someplace warm we can watch the show," he said, and took her hand.

"Where?"

"You'll see when we get there." He led her back into the lodge, through the tangle of confetti and paper streamers fluttering and filling the ballroom. She trusted him and would have followed him just about anywhere, but when they stepped into the empty elevator, she had a suspicion she knew where they were headed, and she didn't like it. When he pushed the number three button, she couldn't help but feel disappointed. What had taken place that afternoon had been a mistake, and one she didn't plan to repeat.

Verdacht

"We won't see anything from my room," she said, looking up into his face, lit by the elevator's fluorescent light.

"That's why we're not going to your room."

"Oh." The doors parted and they stepped into the hall.

Brina followed him past her room to the last door on the left. He slipped his card into the lock, then reached past her and opened the door. From where she stood, Brina could see very little. The room was completely dark, except for the burst of color flashing from outside the windows on the far side of the room and making patterns on the carpet.

except for: außer

"I don't know if this is a good idea," she said, without budging. She was afraid if she walked into the suite, he might assume she wanted to jump in his bed. There were so many reasons why sex with Thomas was a bad idea. Right at the top of the list was the fact that she didn't know how she felt about him, and she certainly didn't know what he felt for her.

without budging: ohne sich von der Stelle zu bewegen

"Why not?"

"Because ..." She paused, trying to think of exactly the right way to phrase what she needed to say, but since she couldn't think of anything, she just blurted out the truth. "I don't want you to think I'm going to have sex with you. After today, you probably assume I do that sort of thing all the time, but I don't."

to phrase: auszudrücken •
just blurted out the truth: platzte sie mit der Wahrheit heraus

"Jesus," he sighed. "First off, I never thought you did. Second, I invited you up here because I thought you might like to watch the show without freezing your

First off: erstens
freezing: abzufrieren

Übung 39

Setzen Sie bitte die Verben in der richtigen Form des Präsens (**present simple** oder **present progressive**) ein.

1. Right now Brina ________________ (to think) of leaving.
2. Brina is sure that she ________________ (to deserve) a trophy, too.
3. She ________________ (to let) her gaze ________________ (to skim) the whole room.
4. While she ________________ (to search) for Karen and Jen, she ________________ (to spot) Thomas.

toes off. And third, I owe you half a bottle of champagne, and I thought you might want it." He paused, then said, "We can go back downstairs if you're uncomfortable."

wenn es dir unangenehm ist

Now she felt stupid. "No, I'd like to stay."

Without turning on the lights, Thomas took her hand. The door slammed shut behind them, and he led her past a grouping of furniture to the windows.

schlug … zu

"Wow," she said as she pulled off her gloves and stuffed them in her pockets. "This is a little bigger than my room."

He moved behind her to help her off with her coat, and when he spoke his voice just seemed to hover in the darkness. "The best part is the Jacuzzi. It seats a family of about six, I think. You'll have to check it out." He walked away with her coat, and Brina couldn't help but wonder if he meant she should check it out as in *look*, or jump inside, by herself or with him. Or if she was reading too much into what he said again.

Whirlpool • ihn testen • konnte nicht umhin • in … hinein-interpretierte •

The lodge sent up another barrage, and Brina's attention was drawn to the fiery corkscrews shooting into the black sky, bursting open like sparkling umbrellas, then falling like rain and hitting the snow beneath.

Leuchtschwall • Korkenzieher • platzten • glitzernde • Schirme

Übung 40 Finden Sie bitte die Wörter auf dieser Doppelseite, die unten umschrieben sind.

1. Large objects in your home ______________

2. The ground you walk on inside a building ______________

3. A TV program with a host and many guests ______________

4. Longer than a jacket and worn in cold weather ______________

5. Made of wool or cotton, it will keep you warm ______________

6. A taste of something to drink ______________

7. A big bathtub with water that bubbles ______________

8. Something you hold over your head when it rains ______________

9. A small object that closes a bottle of champagne ______________

Watching from this side of the lodge was definitely better than standing in the parking lot.
A champagne cork popped and Brina looked over her shoulder to the bar. "I think you definitely have the best seat in the house, Thomas."
She heard his quiet laughter as he approached on silent feet. "Yeah, beats the hell out of freezing like we used to." He handed her a fluted glass. "Happy New Year, Brina."
"Happy New Year." She raised the champagne to her lips and watched him over the top of her glass. Red light flashed across his face and white sweater. "You should be proud of yourself," she said, and took a sip.
"Why?"
"Because you always said you were going to make a million by the time you were thirty. I guess you did it."
"Yes, I did." He drained half his glass as an especially heavy boom filled the air and vibrated the floor beneath their feet. "I've made a lot of money, Brina," he continued when the night fell silent once more. "But it's not the money itself that's important."
He'd been watching too many of those talk shows he'd mentioned. "You sound like Oprah*."

ist verdammt noch mal besser als • Sektglas

Schluck

verdienen

leerte • Knall

10. You wear them over your hands to keep them warm ______

11. An extremely loud noise made by a firecracker __________

12. Area where it is legal to park your car ______________

13. The opposite of upstairs ________________________

14. A house made of wood __________________________

15. Your arms grow out of this part of your body __________

Ophrah Winfrey ist die Moderatorin von The Oprah Winfrey Show, der beliebtesten US-Talkshow.

info

He smiled, his teeth a flash of white between his lips. "That's because Oprah knows."

"What?"

He shrugged. "That it's nice to pay your bills, and it's nice to buy a new coat when you need it, but it can't make you thin, and it can't make you happy."

deine Rechnungen zahlen zu können

Said just like a man who didn't have to worry about paying the bills. "I don't agree. If I was rich, I could hire a chef to cook low fat food all of my life, and I'd buy an ermine coat."

Koch • fettarm • Hermelin • Aschenputtel

"Like Cinderella," he said through his smile.

He remembered. "Yeah, like Cinderella. That would make me damn happy."

"For how long?"

"Forever."

"You're wrong. You can only be Cinderella for so long, then you get bored." He took another drink and looked out the window. "Take it from me, I know."

eine ganze Weile lang

"Money gives you more options," she said as she looked out the window at the brilliant display.

"True, but it can't stop time. You're only given so many days, and when it's your time to check out, money can't stop death and disease. It can buy you the best medical care, but that isn't a guarantee of anything."

Anblick • abzukratzen • Krankheit • ärztliche Versorgung

Übung 41 Beantworten Sie die folgenden Fragen in englischen Sätzen.

1. What did Thomas achieve before he turned thirty?

____

2. Does he have a job at the moment?

____

3. Does he live with his grandparents?

____

4. What is he worried about?

____

5. What are the big things that money can't stop?

____

Her head whipped around and her heart plummeted. "You're not sick, are you?"
"Me?" He shook his head. "No."
"Who are you talking about?"
"No one."
She didn't believe him for a second, but it wasn't real difficult for her to guess who he was thinking about. "You were always a very bad liar. You mentioned your grandfather had health problems. What's wrong?"
"He's old." From beyond the window, an explosion of white lit his profile. "My grandfather's heart has been bad for the last few years. Sometimes when I visit him, his lips turn blue and it scares me shitless. He just pops a little pill and it kick-starts his heart. I've taken him to the best specialist in the country, but he's old and there is nothing anyone can do."
Brina reached for his hand and squeezed. "I'm sorry, Thomas."
"Me too." He raised his glass to his lips and looked over at her. "I've never told anyone about the scaring-me-shitless part. I don't know why I told you."
"Well, I'm glad you did."
His thumb brushed the back of her hand. Another boom and flash, and she watched his gaze drift down her throat to the front of her stretch satin shirt. The explosion from outside faded, and when they were once again pitched in darkness, he asked, "How glad?"
She laughed even as the hair on the back of her neck rose. "Not tear-off-my-clothes glad."
He raised her hand to his mouth and kissed her knuckles. "What would it take to make you tear off your clothes?" The tip of his tongue touched the V of her fingers, sending tingles up her wrist to her elbow.
"I don't think getting naked with you would be a good idea."
"Why not? You didn't seem to mind this afternoon." He turned her hand over and kissed her palm, pausing to suck the very center.

wirbelte herum • sank
Lügner
erhellte
ich mache mir vor Angst in die Hose • wirft … ein • startet … neu
getaucht
reiß-mir-die-Kleider-vom-Leib
genau in der Mitte

"This afternoon was a mistake. You said it yourself. We just got carried away." He blew a breath of warm air into her moist palm and she barely controlled the shiver that raced up her arm. "We should probably just forget that it ever happened."

"Are you going to be able to forget it?"

"I'm going to try. Are you?"

knabberte sich vor bis an • Feuchtigkeit

"No," he said simply, and nibbled his way to her wrist. "Your pulse is racing."

Her hand curled and she held the moisture of his kiss inside. "Thomas?"

"Hmm?"

Ich meine es ernst.

"I'm serious. I don't think this is a good idea."

das … floss • Adern • Ströme • Ausschnitt • Knistern

"You just tell me when you want me to stop," he said, then softly sucked the thin flesh just above her hand. This time she couldn't control the tiny slivers of pleasure tickling her nerve endings, mingling with the blood coursing through her veins. His moist mouth on her sensitive skin sent currents of hot tingles across her breasts and between her thighs. Her nipples drew tight beneath the sheer nylon of her bra, and she thought she should probably tell him to stop now, before he buried his face in her cleavage again. But then the night exploded in a finale of booms and crackles; bursts of color lit the room and Thomas's face. Through the flashes of gold and white, she looked into his eyes. He stared back at her over her wrist, his gaze burning hotter than the flames shooting into the black night. He wanted her. He wanted her as badly as she wanted him. And as she looked into his fiery eyes, she suddenly couldn't remember exactly why making love with Thomas was such a bad idea.

She raised her glass to her lips and drained it. "Why did you dump me today and then go skiing with Holly?"

"I went skiing," he whispered against her skin. "Holly was there. And I didn't dump you. I dropped you off so I could think."

"About?"
Finally he raised his mouth from her. "You," he said, then raised his glass to his lips and drained it.
She didn't know if she believed him completely, but she desperately wanted to. "And what was your conclusion?"
"That I want you, Brina. As badly as I've wanted you for most of my life. Maybe more so now. You're gorgeous and as funny as you always were." He took the glass from her free hand and dropped it, along with his, to the thick carpet where they landed without a sound. "I know why I want you, but I'm just not real certain why you want me."
He couldn't be serious. Not really. "When I first walked into the reunion last night, I thought some lucky girl had hired herself an underwear model to escort her." She looked but could only see the black outline of his face and a splash of dim light provided by a new moon. She wasn't certain, but she thought his brows lowered. "Then Karen told me you were the underwear model, and I was glad. Not just because you look like a guy who should always run around in his BVDs for the enjoyment of women, but because things between us got really bad at the end of high

Schlussfolgerung • sehr

Unterhose

Übung 42

Jeweils zwei Wörter haben eine sehr ähnliche Bedeutung. Ordnen Sie die passenden Wörter einander zu.

1. mad
2. seat
3. zipper
4. partyer
5. chance
6. back
7. shiver
8. shut
9. accompany

☐ guest
☐ shudder
☐ opportunity
☐ spine
☐ closed
☐ chair
☐ escort
☐ angry
☐ button

school, and I was always sorry about what happened."
"What did happen?" he asked, and dropped her hand.
"You know."
"I think I do, but why don't you tell me."
Brina folded her arms beneath her breasts and took a deep breath. "You remember how it was, how I desperately wanted to eat lunch at the big table, to be included with the kids who everyone looked up to. I thought that if Mark liked me, I must be something special." She looked down toward her feet. "No longer munchkin McConnell, the skinny girl whose mother made her clothes."
Thomas placed his fingers beneath her chin and brought her gaze to his. "I liked munchkin McConnell."
"I know, but I didn't."
"What about now? Are you still desperate to sit at the big table?"
"No. I like me."
He brushed his thumb across her lips. "I like you too."
Her lips parted and she licked the pad of his thumb.
"I like your shirt," he said, a catch of desire in his deep voice. "The minute you walked into the banquet room,

Ballen • ein Hauch von Sehnsucht

Übung 43 Im Buchstabendickicht sind horizontal und vertikal englische Wörter aus dem Themenbereich „Geld und Arbeit“ versteckt. Wie viele finden Sie? Kreisen Sie sie ein und notieren Sie sie.

horizontal: ____________________

____

____

____

vertikal: ____________________

____

____

I noticed that shirt." He slid his hand to the back of her neck and pulled her closer.

"It's a nice bright green," she said as she ran her palms up his chest, over the knobby fabric of his sweater.

knubbelig • Pulli

He chuckled. "That isn't what I noticed."

"What then?"

"The way the words *Calvin Klein* stretch across your breasts." He lowered his face and pressed his forehead to hers. "And I wondered how long it was going to take me to get you out of it."

"I thought you invited me up here so my feet wouldn't freeze, and because you owe me half a bottle of champagne."

"That's all true. I just didn't mention that I wanted to eat your shirt off." He pulled her braid over her shoulder and took out the ponytail holder. "I didn't mention that those sparkles in your hair are driving me crazy, and that I want to make love to you with it spread out across my pillow," he said as he unbraided her hair. "That I want to see your face in the morning when I open my eyes." Then he tangled his fingers in her hair and pulled her head back, just as he had that afternoon. And just as earlier, he kissed her parted lips like a man who knew what he wanted and was going

Pferdeschwanz • Spange • ausgebreitet • Kopfkissen • entflocht

es sich nahm

s	b	n	j	o	b	h	n	o	r	k	f	l	a	w	d	r	i	v	e	r	d	w
u	r	o	k	e	s	p	e	c	i	a	l	i	s	t	x	u	l	a	y	f	f	e
p	f	p	o	r	d	e	r	d	f	a	c	d	t	i	h	p	o	u	n	s	k	x
p	e	z	f	l	l	u	h	t	z	b	i	l	l	w	h	r	d	a	p	a	h	i
l	l	e	f	q	u	b	u	s	i	n	e	s	s	d	n	o	e	e	w	l	e	t
i	o	d	i	s	t	e	l	e	p	h	o	n	e	z	l	i	s	e	q	e	k	a
e	u	w	c	o	m	p	u	t	e	r	z	i	k	t	d	e	k	p	t	s	g	i
s	u	l	e	t	e	c	a	y	s	n	o	t	e	s	r	i	z	l	k	e	a	r
J	e	t	t	o	n	w	o	r	k	m	a	n	z	e	r	p	a	y	t	u	x	p
l	t	z	p	p	i	z	y	r	w	d	a	t	i	g	q	x	e	c	l	a	i	m

zog sich zurück • beharrlich • Streicheln • verschlang

after it. His tongue slid inside and withdrew, and he made love to her mouth with hot insistent strokes. He created a wonderfully tight suction and moved his head as he feasted on her lips, his hands opening and closing in her hair.

Brina melted into his chest, the heat of him warming her through his sweater and her shirt, warming her heart deep inside where she'd never been warmed before. He wanted to make love. She wanted that also. She loved Thomas. She's always loved Thomas, only now she'd fallen in love with him too. Her heart and body yearned and ached, and she wanted him the way a woman wanted to be with the man she loved.

sehnte sich • schmerzte

She reached for the end of his sweater and pushed it up his stomach. Her fingers curled into the T-shirt beneath and pushed that up also. And then her hands were on him. On his hot hard flesh and short silky hair. Beneath her touch, his muscles flexed and bunched and she pulled her mouth from his.

spannten sich an • zogen sich zusammen

"Turn on the light", she said. "You got to see me. Now it's my turn. I want to see you."

info

Ein **king-sized bed** entspricht einem Doppelbett von ca. 2 m Breite. Die schmälere Größe ist das **queen-sized bed**, das ungefähr so breit ist wie ein französisches Bett.

Vor allem in den USA ist die internationale Jugendbewegung der Pfadfinder (**Boy Scouts** und **Girl Scouts**) sehr verwurzelt. Bei den uniformierten Pfadfindern lernen Jungen und Mädchen Überlebenstraining, praktische Lebenskenntnisse, Teamarbeit und soziales Engagement. Das Motto der Pfadfinder lautet „Allzeit bereit!". Die Pfadfinderorganisation ist politisch und religiös unabhängig.

Six

Thomas bent at the knees and swung her into his arms. "I know just the place." He carried her as far as the sofa. "Grab my coat," he instructed. When she did, he carried her through the dark suite, through a short hall, and into a pitch black room. He let go of her legs and hit the switch on the wall. Blinding light jabbed Brina's eyes and she buried her face in his neck. "Sorry about that," Thomas said as he dimmed the light.

When her eyes adjusted, she glanced around at the huge room. In the center sat a four-poster king-sized* bed covered with an olive and beige damask spread.

"That bed is huge."

He took the coat from her, and one corner of his mouth lifted into a sensual smile. "Yeah, we'll have to work our way from one end to the other." He dug around in the coat's pocket and pulled out a box of condoms.

"Do you always carry those around in your coat?"

"Nope. I told you I liked that shirt. When you went to sit with your friends," he said as he tossed the box onto a pillow at the head of the bed, "I went to the drugstore."

"Were you so sure of yourself?"

"Where you're concerned?" Thomas walked her backward until the backs of her knees hit the edge of the bed. "Never, but I was a Boy Scout* and I believe in being prepared." She sat and Thomas knelt to remove her boots and socks. He tossed them over his shoulder, and his followed shortly.

"Take your clothes off, Brina," he said as he pushed her down. He moved them to the center of the bed,

let go of: ließ … los • hit: drückte auf • switch: Schalter • jabbed: stach
adjusted: sich daran gewöhnt hatten • four-poster bed: Himmelbett • damask: Damast • spread: Überwurf • sensual: sinnlich
tossed: warf
drugstore: Drogerie
concerned: betrifft
Boy Scout: Pfadfinder • knelt: kniete sich hin
shortly: kurz darauf

then he rolled her on top of him and looked up into her face. “I’ve wanted to say that for a long time.”

Brina sat back across Thomas’s pelvis and crossed her arms over her stomach. She grabbed the end of her shirt and slowly pulled it over her head. She threw it on the floor and tossed her hair over her shoulders. She looked down at him, into his face, his blue eyes burning and heavy. Beneath her, through his jeans and hers, his thick erection pressed into her crotch, long and hard and leaving her wanting even more. Wanting what he could give her, the touch of hot flesh on flesh. She ground against him as he reached for the front closure of her bra. With a twist of his wrist, the clasp opened and he filled his warm palms with her breasts. She shoved her hands beneath his T-shirt and sweater and ran her palms across his belly, just above the waistband of his jeans. He sucked in his breath.

ließ • rieb sich • Verschluss • Haken • Bund • atmete hörbar ein

“You’ve grown a lot more hair than you had in high school.” She ran her hands up the flat muscles of his abdomen to his wide chest. There was no mistaking this man for the skinny kid. “You grew a little taller and bigger.”

Man konnte diesen Mann nicht mit dem dürren Jungen verwechseln.

He grasped her waist and rolled her onto her back. Now it was his turn to straddle her. “I grew bigger everywhere.” He pulled his sweater and T-shirt over his head, balled them up, and tossed them on the floor. “Wanna see, Brina?”

knüllte sie zusammen

She nodded and touched him wherever her hands landed. His thighs, waist, and hard corrugated belly. Short black curls grew across his chest, and in a thin line down his sternum to his navel. Within the dimmed light of the bedroom, his eyes seemed brighter. They burned and her heart fluttered, her pulse erratic. “Are we going to play show and tell*?”

gewellt • Locken • Brustbein • unregelmäßig

He shook his head and lowered his face to her right breast. “We’re going to play ‘I’ll show you mine if you show me yours.'" He stroked her nipple with his tongue until it turned hard, then he gazed up into her face and sucked her wet nipple into his mouth.

She ran her fingers through the hair on the side of his head, the pleasure so delicious, the heat of his mouth so exquisite her back arched off the mattress. She ran her hands down his sides to his waist, then up and down his thighs as far as she could reach. Her fingers spread wide, and her thumbs pressed into his erection. He kissed between her breasts, his short breaths heating her already hot skin. Then he stood on his knees. Cool air brushed across her wet nipples as she looked up into his face, and she reached for the first metal button closing the waistband of his Levi's. She rose onto one elbow, then pushed herself until she sat between his thighs. As she popped all five buttons, she leaned forward and kissed his navel.

Thomas took a deep breath and held it. She kissed his belly, the fine hair of his treasure trove, and the elastic band of his briefs. "I read somewhere," she whispered as she slid her hands around his sides and slipped them beneath his jeans and underwear, "that a woman should never give a man oral pleasure on their

köstlich

Schatzkammer • Gummiband • Slip

Oralsex

info

Show and tell ist ein fester Bestandteil des Unterrichts an amerikanischen Grundschulen. Die Schüler bringen z. B. ihr Haustier mit in den Unterricht und vermitteln so der Klasse nützliche Informationen über das Tier, seine Pflege etc. Dabei entwickeln sie die Fähigkeit des freien Vortragens und Präsentierens.

Ein gängiger Kalauer unter Liebespaaren ist der Vorschlag to play show and tell, um sich näherzukommen.

Übung 44

Ergänzen Sie die fehlenden Buchstaben des gesuchten Begriffs.

The New Year starts at the s _ _ _ _ _ of m _ _ _ _ _ _ _.

first date." She grasped his tight bare behind and squeezed.

"This isn't our first date," he said, his voice raw.

She hooked her thumbs beneath his jeans and briefs and slowly slid them down his thighs. Brina stared at him, fascinated by the pubic hair that grew denser on his groin. His penis jutted toward her, thick with his flagrant arousal. She wrapped her hand around his hard shaft, stroking his engorged flesh and feeling the incredible heat of him. "The article said it will scare a man away and he'll never call again." She raised her gaze to his face, and asked, "Are you scared?"

He shook his head. "Only that you'll leave."

"Good answer," she said, and brought him to her mouth. She licked the clear seminal bead resting in the cleft of his plump head. A ragged moan was torn from his throat as she opened her mouth and sucked him inside. Her tongue licked and tortured him until he pushed her away. His breath rough and heavy, his eyes dark blue slits of desire, he tore at his jeans and tugged at hers until they were both naked, the hard points of her breasts pressing into his chest. Their legs entwined, his mouth feeding off hers, their hot bodies locked in passion. His hand moved down her

steckte

Schamhaar • zeigte • offenkundig • Erregung • Schaft • streichelte • prall • unglaublich

Samentropfen • Spalte • Eichel

Schlitze • zerrte • Spitzen • umschlangen einander • verschlang • verschmolzen

Übung 45 Welche Satzteile passen zusammen? Tragen Sie bitte die entsprechenden Buchstaben in die Kästchen ein.

1. Brina came back to her hometown
2. Her best friend, Stephanie, stayed at home
3. Thomas Mack was surprised
4. One of the trophies Mindy handed out was
5. Brina felt uncomfortable
6. Brina was bored with Mark's friends
7. The reunion was moved to a banquet room
8. Brina stayed at the back of the room

side and slid between her legs, his fingers touching and stroking her slick flesh. Brina moaned deep in her throat.

stöhnte

"What did the article say about women?" he asked as he tore his mouth from hers. "Do women get scared?"

It took her a moment to understand what he was asking. She didn't want to climax that way. She wanted to come with him deep inside her. She was already so close, she squeezed her thighs around his pleasure-giving hand to stop him. "It didn't say." She licked her moist lips. They felt swollen and her voice sounded drugged when she said, "Make love to me." She reached over her head for the box of condoms, then pushed Thomas to his back. While he watched she stretched the thin latex and unrolled it down his hard thick shaft to his dark pubic hair. Then she was on her back looking up at him, his knees between her thighs, the head of his penis touching her inner thigh.

zum Höhepunkt kommen • kurz davor

wie unter Drogen

"This could get rough," he warned as he pushed inside.

She couldn't help her sigh of pleasure as he slipped more deeply into her.

a) because she had just given birth to a baby.
b) for having the most freckles.
c) when Holly completely ignored her.
d) because they had not evolved that much.
e) because she had received an invitation to a class reunion.
f) because the lodge was hosting its annual New Year's Eve party.
g) so she could make a quiet exit just in case she felt like it.
h) that Brina had changed so much in the past ten years.

Unterarme He rested his weight on his forearms, and his hands held her face. Looking deep into her eyes, he moved within her body, touching and stroking the exact place where her pleasure was centered, in and out, driving her wild with the need of him. Withdrawing slowly and plunging deep. And with each stroke, pushing, building, toward climax.

dem Verlangen nach ihm • Eintauchen • Höhepunkt

She slid her hands down the contours of his back to the hard cheeks of his behind. "Faster," she whispered against his mouth. She moved with him as he pumped his hips harder, deeper, faster. Heat and desire, flushing her skin and tangling her nerves into hot twisted knots. She, too, moved her hands to his face and she looked into his eyes. "Thomas," she moaned as he drove into her, pushing her harder, higher. "I love you." She gasped as an orgasm gripped her insides with intense pleasure. It ripped through her, again and again, her body pulsing around him as he thrust into her over and over, driving her farther up the bed. Then his fingers on the sides of her face curled, and his climax tore a deep primal groan from his chest that seemed to last forever.

Umriss • Pobacken • bewegte • in sie eindrang • packte • intensiv • immer wieder • animalisch • Stöhnen

"Brina," he said on a harsh exhalation as his hips stilled. He stared into her eyes, his breathing harsh,

Ausatmen

Übung 46 Welche der drei Aussagen ist die richtige? Kreuzen Sie sie an.

1. When Brina walked into the reunion on the first night, she thought
- ☐ Thomas was an underwear model a girl had hired to escort her.
- ☐ Thomas was a lingerie model a girl had hired to escort her.
- ☐ Thomas wasn't wearing any underwear.

2. Brina thinks Thomas
- ☐ should always run around without wearing any underwear.
- ☐ looks like a guy who should always run around in his underwear.
- ☐ looks like a guy who enjoys women.

then he pushed deep into her one last time and stayed there. "Are you okay?" he asked.

She was more than okay, and smiled. "I'm great."

"Yes, you are." He kissed her eyebrows and her nose. "Any friction burns?"

She tilted her head back and noticed the close proximity of the headboard. "Not that I know of."

"I can check it out for you in a minute," he said as he withdrew from her. "I'll be right back."

He left her and walked into the bathroom. Brina rolled onto her stomach and pressed her cheek against the cool damask fabric. She'd told him she loved him. He hadn't said anything.

"Hey," he called from the other room. "If you're hungry, we can raid the bar. It's stocked with some pretty good stuff."

And raid it, they did. They ate crackers and cheese and opened a tin of cured ham. For dessert they had truffles and chocolate-covered macadamia nuts. They made love on the floor behind the bar and in the Jacuzzi as the hot water swirled around their naked bodies.

Thomas never mentioned the word *love* in the context of loving her, but he touched her as if he did. He carefully dried her skin with a thick towel and combed the tangles from her wet hair.

No, when he mentioned the word, he said things like, "I've always loved your hair. I could do this forever." And "I'd love for you to see my condo. Aspen is beautiful."

Somewhere around 4:00 A.M. he walked her down the hall to her room.

"Are you sure you won't come back to bed with me?" Thomas asked as he stuck her key card in the lock. "I want to sleep with you." He opened the door and yawned. "Just sleep, I promise."

And wake up with bed head and morning breath? No way. "Call me when you wake up," she said as she slid

Reibungswunden • Nähe • Kopfteil

plündern • gefüllt • Und sie plünderten sie in der Tat. • Dose • gepökelt • in Schokolade gehüllt • sprudelte • im Zusammenhang mit

ich möchte gerne, dass du

gähnte • zerknautscht • Mundgeruch • auf keinen Fall

her hands up his chest and rose onto her toes. With her heart thumping in her chest, she wrapped her arms around his neck and kissed him good night. She'd never felt the way she did at that exact moment. Excited, euphoric, utterly happy. Maybe because she'd never loved a man the way she loved Thomas Mack.

sie hatte sich noch nie so gefühlt wie • vollkommen

When Brina woke later that morning, the light on her telephone flashed. It was eleven-thirty and Thomas obviously hadn't called. He was probably still asleep.

blinkte

She picked up the receiver, dialed for her message, then laid her head on her pillow and listened.

Hörer • Nachricht

"Brina, it's Thomas. Something came up and I need to leave immediately. It's six-thirty and I didn't want to wake you up, but ... Listen, I'm driving straight through to Denver and catching a plane to Palm Springs. I don't know when ..." He sighed. "I'll talk to you when I get a chance."

abfahren • sofort • nehme • Flieger

Brina listened to the message three more times before she hung up the telephone. He was gone. He'd just left. He'd left without pounding on her door to talk to her. He'd left without mentioning when she might see him again. He'd left without telling her he loved her or kissing her good-bye.

hämmern

Brina pushed her hair out of her face and shoved her legs into her jeans. She called the front desk and asked if he'd left her a message.

He hadn't.

Wearing an old sweatshirt and her jeans, she grabbed her key card and headed down the hall. The door to Thomas's room was open and the maid cart was just inside. Brina walked into the room and glanced around. The furniture had been polished, the carpet vacuumed, and the bar restocked. She moved to the doorway of the bedroom and stopped. Two maids were in the process of fitting the bed with new sheets.

Wagen des Zimmermädchens • gesaugt • wieder aufgefüllt • das Bett zu beziehen

All traces of him were gone. His clothes, the sheets he'd slept on, the towels he'd used to dry her off.

Spuren

One of the maids looked up. "Can I help you?"

Brina shook her head. "No, thanks," she said, and turned away. He was truly gone, and until that moment, she hadn't realized she was holding her breath, hanging on to the hope that it was a mistake. That he was just down the hall waiting for her.

dass sie den Atem anhielt • sich an die Hoffnung klammerte

She walked back to her room and stuck her card in the lock. He'd said he was flying out of Denver to Palm Springs. That was where his grandparents lived. Something really bad must have happened.

I'll talk to you when I get a chance, he'd said.

Brina sat on the corner of her bed and stared at the blank screen of the television. She remembered when Thomas's dog, Scooter, had died, and he'd tried to be real stoic. He hadn't cried, even though she'd known he wanted to. He'd held it in, his cheeks red with the effort. He hadn't wanted her around then, and he obviously didn't want her around now. If he did, he would have at least left a number where she could reach him. Of course, she could track him down. After all, that was what she did for a living. She could walk right downstairs and ask Mindy for a copy of his reunion

leer • Bildschirm • gelassen • hatte sich zurückgehalten • Anstrengung • erreichen • finden • womit sie ihr Geld verdiente

Übung 47

Welcher Satz passt zu welcher Formulierung? Tragen Sie die Buchstaben in die richtigen Kästchen ein.

1. ☐ She will never do that.	a) to talk yourself out of sth.
2. ☐ He swallowed his pain.	b) to rather eat worms
3. ☐ She lost control of herself.	c) to pay attention
4. ☐ Then she had an idea.	d) to get carried away
5. ☐ He is dying to know.	e) to hold it in
6. ☐ She kept from laughing.	f) to come up with something
7. ☐ He listened closely.	g) to keep a straight face
8. ☐ He dropped his plan.	h) to definitely want to find out

Anmeldeformular • Demütigung • vorziehen • vermeiden • Stolz • um auf … zu kommen • Kennzeichen

registration form. Then Mindy would know he hadn't given her his address or telephone number. That was one humiliation Brina would prefer to avoid. She was desperate to talk to him, but she did have her pride.

It took her a day to come up with Thomas's address in Aspen. She'd remembered part of the license plate number of his Jeep, and she'd contacted the Department of Motor Vehicles in Colorado several times before getting what she wanted. Now all she needed was his telephone number. Since she lived in Oregon, she couldn't exactly run down to her local telephone company and scan their files. She didn't know anyone who worked for the phone company in Aspen, and she'd have to get a court order.

durchsuchen • Unterlagen • richterliche Verfügung • finden • zog das große Los • Telefonbuch • stellte … Nachforschungen an

She turned her attention to locating his grandparents and hit the jackpot. Not only were they listed in the telephone directory, she made several inquiries at the hospitals in and around Palm Springs and discovered that Thomas's grandfather had been transferred to a hospital in Rancho Mirage.

By the third day after the reunion, Brina had the address and telephone number of not only his grandparents, but him as well.

Übung 48 Bitte wählen Sie das jeweils richtige Wort aus und unterstreichen Sie es.

1. The (more / most / least) Brina thought about it, the (angry / angrier / angriest) she became.
2. Brina got an award for having changed (the more / much / the most).
3. Thomas had earned (some / many / a lot of) money before his thirtieth birthday.
4. Some of the guests were already (near / nearly / close) drunk.
5. The (less / lesser / least) she thought about Thomas, the (good / well / better) she'd feel.

I'll talk you when I get a chance, he'd said, and she was beginning to believe he hadn't meant it. That he was blowing her off.
She had his number in a folder on her desk, right next to her regular cases. She sat back in her chair and looked out her office window onto the street below. It was raining. So what was new?
Droplets hit the tinted glass at an angle and ran in a squiggly pattern to the metal sill below. Now that she had the information she needed, she was reluctant to use it. It had been three days and Thomas hadn't tried to contact her. She checked her answering machine at home about every half hour. The fact that he didn't have her home telephone number didn't keep her from checking. She instructed her assistant that if a man called for her, she was to put him directly through. Each time the phone rang, her heart leapt and her pulse raced and it was never Thomas.
Brina slipped off her five-inch heels and turned toward her desk. She opened a report on a workmen's comp claim she was investigating. She only read about two paragraphs of the report until her mind once again returned to Thomas.
She was afraid. More afraid than she'd ever been in her

ernst gemeint • sie sausen ließ • Ordner • Schreibtisch

Wie üblich. • Tröpfchen • getönt • schräg • schnörkelig • Sims • sträubte sie sich • Anrufbeantworter

sollte sie ihn direkt durchstellen • schlug höher • Pumps mit 12 cm hohen Absätzen • Abschnitte

Übung 49

Was ist an den folgenden Aussagen falsch? Bitte streichen Sie das falsche Wort durch und korrigieren Sie den Satz.

1. Brina woke early that morning. ______
2. Thomas left a written message for Brina. ______
3. He would be driving straight through to Denver and catching a plane in Palm Springs. ______
4. Brina called the front desk at her office. ______
5. Then she headed downstairs. ______
6. The maid cart was in the hall. ______
7. The furniture was just being polished by two maids.

______

life. What if he didn't want to talk to her or see her? What if he felt nothing for her? She was on an emotional roller coaster. Up and down. Her heart speeding at the memory of his kiss, slowing with the thought of never seeing him again. Her emotions were a chaotic mess, and she didn't know what to do about it. One second she thought she should call him, but in the next, she reminded herself that he'd said he would call her when he got the chance.

"I was hoping you could help me." The voice startled her and she glanced up.

Slowly she closed the file and looked into Thomas's blue eyes. At the sight of him, her heart skidded to a stop. He wore a charcoal suit over a black turtleneck. In his hands he held three small bouquets of roses. Tight buds of red, white, and yellow. "Help you with what?" she asked.

He walked into the office and stopped on the other side of her desk. "I was hoping you could help me find someone."

"Who?"

"A girl I graduated high school with. She dumped me for a jerk, but I thought I'd give her a chance to make it up."

Achterbahn • Durcheinander • erschreckte • sah auf • blieb ihr Herz stehen • dunkelgrau • Rollkragenpulli • Sträuße • dicht • Knospen • Idiot • es wieder gutzumachen

info Die Südstaaten der USA (wie zum Beispiel Mississippi, Alabama, Georgia, Florida usw.) gelten im Vergleich zum Norden als etwas rückständiger. Noch heute bestehen dort strengere und zum Teil veraltete Gesetze.

Übung 50 Bitte setzen Sie im folgenden if-Satz Typ II (Vergangenheit) die beiden Infinitive in Klammern in der korrekten Form ein.

1. If she ____________________ (to ask) Mindy for Thomas's phone number, Mindy ____________________ (to know) that he had not given Brina his address.

Brina tried not to smile. He was here, in her office, and everything suddenly felt right in her life. The backs of her eyes stung. "What did you have in mind and is it legal?" brannten

"Probably not in some of those southern states*."

She stood and walked about the corner of her desk. "How did you find me?" she asked. lief um … herum

"I called Mindy Burton."

Of course. "How's your grandfather?"

"Not good." His brows lowered over beautiful blue eyes. "But I don't want to talk about that now. We can talk about that later if you want. Right now I want to talk about something that makes sense to me. I want to talk about us." He handed her the flowers. "The florist told me that red roses symbolize passionate love, white, pure love, and yellow, friendship." überreichte • leidenschaftlich • rein •

She held them up to her nose and inhaled deeply. "They're gorgeous, Thomas." She blinked to hold back her tears. "Thank you." atmete … ein

"First we were friends and then lovers," he said. "I want us to continue to be friends and lovers."

Brina laid the flowers on the desk and stepped into his waiting arms. "I want that, too."

"Do you remember Saturday when I told you that we didn't know each other anymore?"

She nodded and buried her face in his chest. She breathed deep. Breathing in the scent of the man she loved with her heart and soul.

"Well, that wasn't true then and it isn't true now. I know you, Brina. I know when you're going to cry, and I know when you're going to laugh. What's going to make you happy or sad or angry. It's been ten years, but I know you." He kissed the top of her head. "And I've missed you."

"I missed you, too." She leaned forward and softly kissed his mouth.

His hands moved up to the sides of her head and he held her face in his palms. Holding her away. "But I want more than love and friendship," he said. "I tried to tell myself that I didn't go to the reunion looking for you, but I did. I lied about that, and I lied a little bit about the roses too. The white roses don't just mean pure love. They mean pure love in marriage." He looked deeply into her eyes and said, "I want to be with you forever. I love you."

sammelten sich The tears she'd tried to hold back gathered on her bottom lashes. "I love you, too."

He wiped the moisture away with his thumbs. "That's what I needed to hear."

"I told you I loved you the other night. Did you hear me?"

"Yes." He looked into her eyes and said through a smile, "But we were making love, and I didn't know if you meant it or if you were just, you know, carried away."

"I did mean it."

Slowly he lowered his head and pressed his mouth to hers. A gentle hello kiss that lasted about three seconds before it turned hot and energetic. As if to reassure herself, Brina ran her hands over him. (sanft • energisch)

He pulled back and took several deep breaths. "My life is a mess right now. My grandfather is dying and there is nothing I can do but sit by his side and watch it happen. Everything I own is in Colorado, I'm living with my grandmother in Palm Springs, and I'm currently unemployed. Everything in my life right now is uncertain except how I feel about you. You are the only thing that feels right to me. I know this may sound crazy, but I'm asking anyway. Come be with me." (zurzeit)

stieß … hervor Shocked, Brina uttered, "Where?"

"For now, somewhere in Palm Springs. Later, who knows? Wherever you want." (wo immer)

Brina raised her brows up her forehead. "When?"

"Right now. Today. Tomorrow. Next week. Next month." He shook his head. "Whenever you're able. I'm asking you to marry me. To be with me now and (wann immer) forever. I know it might sound like a hasty, irrational decision, but I've waited for you since the first grade." Brina smiled. It didn't sound hasty or irrational at all. Not to her. "I'll be your friend, your lover, and your wife. I'll marry you today. Tomorrow. Next week. Next month." She pressed her forehead to his. "I want to be with you now and forever."

hasty – übereilt
wife – Ehefrau

Übung 51

Welches Wort passt nicht zu den anderen in der Reihe? Unterstreichen Sie es.

1. stare, see, recognize, watch, look
2. devour, drink, binge, purge, eat
3. toe, thump, wrist, knuckle, arm
4. pants, dress, top, suite, coat
5. purse, belt, foot, watch, shoes
6. umbrella, snow, ski, boots, lift
7. slide, glide, skid, smooth, stop
8. jealous, angry, embarrassed, mad, loved

Lösungen

1 The **itinerary** had **indicated semiformal** dress for the **cocktail** party, and Brina's **sleeveless** red dress was **perfect**.

2
1. [X] **Brina has long brown hair.**
Brina hat langes braunes Haar.
2. [ ] She is usually not pleased with the way she looks.
Meistens findet sie sich nicht schön.
3. [ ] She is flat-chested and skinny.
Sie hat keinen Busen und ist dünn.
4. [X] **Brina works in Portland.**
Brina arbeitet in Portland.
5. [ ] The school reunion will be over Sunday night.
Das Klassentreffen endet Sonntagabend.
6. [ ] The small town of Galliton Pass is a summer resort.
Die Kleinstadt Galliton Pass ist im Sommer ein Touristenort.
7. [ ] Brina comes from a rich family.
Brina kommt aus einer reichen Familie.
8. [X] **Brina's friend Stephanie stayed at home with her baby.**
Brinas Freundin Stephanie ist mit ihrem Baby zu Hause geblieben.
9. [ ] Brina is a police investigator.
Brina ist Kriminalbeamtin.

3
1. husband, wife, **marriage**, spouse
2. photo, picture, drawing, **vision**
3. **blackboard**, teacher, pupil, graduate
4. suit, **purse**, jacket, trousers
5. **insured**, unsure, insecure, sure
6. jaw, **flaw**, butt, cheek
7. unruly, gangly, **really**, wavy

4
1. **He was inspecting her instead of checking her out.**
2. **The blue tie was held in place by a gold clasp.**
3. **They'd gotten drunk on Karen's daddy's homemade wine.**
4. **Brina had only had two serious relationships since high school.**
5. **Neither relationship had lasted more than a few years.**
6. **Crowds were reliving their high school glory days.**
7. **Brina didn't bother to look at the pictures.**

5

1. Brina had **grown** into more of a woman than the girl he'd known.
2. The stranger's eyes **moved** to her hips and legs.
3. Probably some girl had **begged** a hunky guy to escort her tonight.
4. "Who **did** you marry?"
5. He had **bought** her a blue Popsicle that **had** cost him a quarter.
6. She didn't **know** how to respond to that.

6

lawyer	**justice**
driver	**race car**
consultant	**advice**
doctor	**patient**
investigator	**crime**
homemaker	**family**
trombonist	**music**
salesman	**product**
teacher	**student**
model	**clothing**

7

1. Thomas polished off his **drink**.
2. He didn't need to beat his **chest**.
3. He just had a different sense of **humor**.
4. His former girlfriend modeled **lingerie** for an American company.
5. Thomas spotted Brina the **second** she walked into the room.
6. Brina sighed on a breathless little **laugh**.
7. Then she made an effort at **conversation**.

8

1. effort	**ease**
2. tuxedo	**dress**
3. rumor	**fact**
4. Democrat	**Republican**
5. hell	**heaven**
6. latter	**former**
7. funeral	**birth**
8. investigator	**criminal**
9. pleasure	**discomfort**
10. chest	**back**

9

1. to transform: **transformation**
2. to disappoint: **disappointment**
3. to think: **thought**
4. to resemble: **resemblance**
5. to return: **return**
6. to remember: **memory** (oder: **remembrance**)
7. to announce: **announcement**
8. to care: **care**
9. to impress: **impression**
10. to enjoy: **enjoyment**

10 **1.** impeccable
2. classmates
3. lodge
4. pregnant
5. sophomore
6. fraud
7. divorced
8. unwritten rule

11 **1.** All she had to do was snap her fingers. / She only had to snap her fingers.
Sie brauchte bloß mit den Fingern zu schnippen.
2. He calls himself a moron.
Er nennt sich einen Idioten.
3. She describes (the old) Holly as a walking, talking Malibu Barbie doll.
Sie beschreibt (die frühere) Holly als eine laufende und sprechende Malibu-Barbiepuppe.

12 **1.** When her gaze returned to his, he asked, "What are you looking for, Brina?"
2. "You," she answered. "I'm wondering if I know you anymore."
3. Everyone clapped except Brina. She couldn't. She had a glass in her hand. Thomas didn't applaud either.
4. "George Bush was sworn in as the forty-first president(,) and Lucille Ball died at the age of seventy-seven," Mindy continued.
5. With his drink in one hand, phone in the other, Thomas left.

13 **1.** The inside of your hand is called your palm.
Die Innenseite der Hand wird Handfläche genannt.
2. Please don't dig me in the ribs with your elbow!
Bitte stich mir deinen Ellbogen nicht in die Rippen!
3. The stranger's gaze lingered on her big breasts.
Der Blick des Fremden blieb an ihren üppigen Brüsten hängen.
4. Thomas held her close to his muscular chest.
Thomas drückte sie fest an seine muskulöse Brust.
5. She felt butterflies in her stomach.
Sie spürte Schmetterlinge im Bauch.
6. Looking at her, he lifted a brow.
Er sah sie an und zog die Augenbraue hoch.
7. Thomas had beautiful eyes with long black lashes.
Thomas hatte schöne Augen mit langen schwarzen Wimpern.
8. He put his hand on her shoulder and started to dance with her.
Er legte die Hand auf ihre Schulter und fing an, mit ihr zu tanzen.

14 **1.** No one was interested in what Mindy had to say.
2. Brina arrived in Galliton Pass in the evening.
3. Mark told Brina about the businesses he owns.
4. Watching Thomas dance with Holly, Brina felt jealous.
5. When Brina joined the Ski Club, she broke her leg.

15 **1.** Brina woke the next morning feeling tired.
2. She had ended up at Mark's house with a bunch of his friends.
3. His friends had not evolved that much.
4. Brina had been awake all night.
5. She had become so angry at Thomas that she would have liked to punch him.
6. At eight-thirty in the morning she was exhausted.
7. She dialled room service.

16 **body parts:** buns, teeth, fingertip, waist, elbow, throat, toe
dress: swimsuit, panties, belt, sleeves, pants, robe, pocket
hotel: curtains, elevator, towel, shower, chandelier, tray, room service

17 **1.** die Vergangenheit aufarbeiten
2. sich auf den Weg zur Tür machen
3. in einer Bar rumhängen

18 **1.** mechanic
2. silk
3. chess
4. coconut
5. guitar
6. embarrassment
7. doll
8. hazel
9. spear

19 **1.** Brina moved her palm across his shoulder.
2. She might hang out at the lodge.
3. Thomas blew into the cup of hot coffee.
4. The heat from his body was still warming her fingertips.
5. She was dying of embarrassment.
6. He glanced at his wristwatch.
7. He walked out of the room and into the hall.
8. His skis leaned against the fireplace.

20
1. Die Leute (da) unten sahen aus wie bunte Ameisen.
2. Die kalte Luft war vom Geräusch des Kabels erfüllt.
3. Seine Wangen fingen an, rosa zu werden./Seine Wangen erröteten langsam.
4. Ihre Pupillen zogen sich zusammen und sie senkte den Blick.
5. Brina folgte der Frau/observierte die Frau ungefähr drei Wochen lang.
6. Sie fotografierte die Antragstellerin dabei, wie sie/diese mit ihren Kindern Boxauto fuhr.
7. Brina wandte den Blick ab und sah hinunter auf die Baumwipfel.
8. Sie fragte sich, wie es sich (wohl) anfühlen würde, ihn zu küssen.
9. Früher verabreichte Brina Thomas immer „Medizinpulver“, das sie aus zermahlenen Smarties hergestellt hatte.

21
1. The sky was almost cloudless and Thomas was dressed completely in black.
2. Getting on the ski lift was easier than she had thought.
3. They had not seen each other for ten years.
4. Brina was no longer as skinny as she had been during her high school years.

22
1. A long reptile without any feet is called a snake.
2. A shot is medicine given with a needle.
3. The landscape or sky behind an object is called the backdrop.
4. You need to keep your balance so you won't fall.
5. Thirty degrees Fahrenheit is freezing cold.
6. Sports jackets often close with a zip.

23

	5									6				7
1	d	i	s	a	p	p	o	i	n	t	m	e	n	t
2	r	e	a	l	l	y				r				e
	i									o				m
	v									m				p
3	e	a	s	e	l					b				l
	w									o				e
	a									n				
4	y	e	l	l						e				

24
1. feet
2. teeth
3. wrists
4. babies
5. women
6. kisses
7. wristwatches
8. boots
9. halves
10. trays

25 **1.** **She paid for her ski equipment by saving all her babysitting money.**
Sie bezahlte ihre Skiausrüstung, indem sie das ganze Geld vom Babysitten sparte.
2. **She broke her leg on her first day of skiing.**
Sie brach sich das Bein am ersten Tag, an dem sie Ski fuhr.
3. **Mark and his friends played a trick on the Chess Club by hiding all the kings.**
Mark und seine Freunde spielten dem Schachklub einen Streich, indem sie alle Könige versteckten.
4. **Holly wears a skintight stretch one-piece (suit).**
Holly trägt einen hautengen Stretch-Einteiler.

26 **1.** **A skintight ski suit is worn by Holly.**
2. **Brina is being taught by Thomas how to ski.**
3. **A computer software company was started by Thomas five years ago.**
4. **Brina was tormented by Holly in high school.**

27 **1.** **I believe, I think**
2. **I guess, I figure**
3. **I bet**
4. **I feel**
5. **I assume**
6. **I'm kidding**

28 **1.** **Brina is afraid of falling in love with Thomas.**
Brina befürchtet, sie könnte sich in Thomas verlieben.
2. **Thomas ignored Holly's offer to have sex with her.**
Thomas ignorierte Hollys Angebot, mit ihr zu schlafen.
3. **Thomas doesn't care how much a bottle of champagne costs.**
Thomas ist es egal, wie viel eine Flasche Champagner kostet.
4. **Both have lost half the bet.**
Beide haben die Wette halb verloren.
5. **Thomas knows how to seduce women.**
Thomas weiß, wie man Frauen verführt.

29 **1.** She **had leaned** forward.
2. She **will taste** his skin.
3. He **bent** his knees.
4. He **is going to grab** the backs of her thighs.
5. She **feels** him through the thin material of her suit.
6. He **will have kissed** the hollow of her throat.

30 **For Brina men were like food to binge on.**
Für Brina waren Männer wie Essen, das man gierig verschlang.

31
1. **to undress**
2. **rich**
3. **insignificant**
4. **front yard**
5. **employed**
6. **ugly**
7. **fat**
8. **bottom**
9. **soft; gentle**
10. **king**
11. **noise**
12. **to raise**
13. **married; single**

32 **All day Thomas had pictured Brina wearing long johns. / All day Thomas had pictured Brina in long johns.**

33
1. Now Brina was older and **wiser**.
2. She was fairly **picky** about whom she let worship her body.
3. She had to feel **comfortable** with a man before becoming **intimate** with him.
4. Everything was **different** today – turned **upside** down and inside **out**.

34
1. **reproductive organ**
2. **misconstrued**
3. **annual**
4. **quiet**
5. **cheerful**
6. **casual**
7. **motive**

35
1. Brina is **jealous of** Holly dancing with Thomas.
   Brina ist auf Holly, die mit Thomas tanzt, eifersüchtig.
2. She is **afraid of** falling in love with him.
   Sie hat Angst davor, sie könnte sich in ihn verlieben.
3. Brina is **confused about** her desire to make love to him.
   Brina ist über ihre Sehnsucht, mit ihm zu schlafen, verwirrt.
4. She is **uncertain about** his true feelings.
   Sie ist sich seiner wahren Gefühle nicht sicher.
5. She is **annoyed at** the lame committee.
   Sie ärgert sich über das lahme Komitee.

36
1. **to flood**
2. **to worship**
3. **to express**
4. **to laugh**
5. **to excuse**
6. **to gaze**
7. **to seat**
8. **to invite**

37
1. All of the guests are **invited** to join the celebration.
2. The lodge will ring **in** the New Year.
3. Five minutes before midnight a **complimentary glass of champagne** will be provided.
4. **Some** of the guests will be first in line to take advantage of free alcohol.
5. A few classmates had already **drunk** too much.
6. They were obviously well **past** three sheets.
7. They will get together in the ballroom for **their** farewell brunch.
8. Brina wondered what **could possibly** outdo cheap trophies.
9. She had always loved to watch the fireworks being shot **into** the sky.
10. She had had to watch **from** the parking lot.

38
1. **nail**
2. **finger**
3. **knuckle**
4. **wrist**
5. **thumb**
6. **palm**

39
1. Right now Brina **is thinking** of leaving.
2. Brina is sure that she **deserves** a trophy, too.
3. She **lets** her gaze **skim** the whole room.
4. While she **is searching** for Karen and Jen, she **spots** Thomas.

40
1. furniture
2. floor
3. talk show
4. coat
5. sweater
6. sip
7. Jacuzzi
8. umbrella
9. cork
10. gloves
11. boom
12. parking lot
13. downstairs
14. lodge
15. shoulders

41
1. He made a million dollars.
   Er hat eine Million Dollar verdient.
2. No, currently / at the moment he is unemployed.
   Nein, zurzeit ist er arbeitslos.
3. No, he lives in his condo.
   Nein, er wohnt in seiner Eigentumswohnung.
4. He is worried about his grandfather's health.
   Er macht sich Sorgen um die Gesundheit seines Großvaters.
5. Money can't stop time, death and disease.
   Geld kann nicht die Zeit, den Tod und Krankheit aufhalten.

42

1. mad	angry
2. seat	chair
3. zipper	bullon
4. partyer	guest
5. chance	opportunity
6. back	spine
7. shiver	shudder
8. shut	closed
9. accompany	escort

43 horizontal: **job, driver, specialist, order, bill, business, telephone, computer, notes, workman, pay, claim.**
vertikal: **supplies, office, desk, sales.**

s	b	n	j	o	b	h	n	o	r	k	f	l	a	w	d	r	i	v	e	r	d	w
u	r	o	k	e	s	p	e	c	i	a	l	i	s	t	x	u	l	a	y	f	f	e
p	f	p	o	r	d	e	r	d	f	a	c	d	t	i	h	p	o	u	n	s	k	x
p	e	z	f	l	l	u	h	t	z	b	i	l	l	w	h	r	d	a	p	a	h	i
l	l	e	f	q	u	b	u	s	i	n	e	s	s	d	n	o	e	e	w	l	e	t
i	o	d	i	s	t	e	l	e	p	h	o	n	e	z	l	i	s	e	q	e	k	a
e	u	w	c	o	m	p	u	t	e	r	z	i	k	t	d	e	k	p	t	s	g	i
s	u	l	e	t	e	c	a	y	s	n	o	t	e	s	r	i	z	l	k	e	a	r
J	e	t	t	o	n	w	o	r	k	m	a	n	z	e	r	p	a	y	t	u	x	p
l	t	z	p	p	i	z	y	r	w	d	a	t	i	g	q	x	e	c	l	a	i	m

44 The New Year starts at the **stroke** of **midnight**.

45 **1.e)** Brina came back to her hometown **because she had received an invitation to a class reunion.**
Brina war in ihren Heimatort zurückgekommen, weil sie eine Einladung zu einem Klassentreffen erhalten hatte.

2.a) Her best friend, Stephanie, stayed at home **because she had just given birth to a baby.**
Ihre beste Freundin Stephanie blieb zuhause, weil sie gerade ein Baby zur Welt gebracht hatte.

3.h) Thomas Mack was surprised **that Brina had changed so much in the past ten years.**
Thomas Mack war erstaunt, dass Brina sich in den letzten zehn Jahren so verändert hatte.

4.b) One of the trophies Mindy handed out was **for having the most freckles.**
Eine der Trophäen, die Mindy verteilte, war für die meisten Sommersprossen.

5.c) Brina felt uncomfortable **when Holly completely ignored her.**
Brina fühlte sich unbehaglich, als Holly sie völlig ignorierte.

6.d) Brina was bored with Mark's friends **because they had not evolved that much.**
Brina langweilte sich mit Marks Freunden, da diese sich nicht sonderlich weiterentwickelt hatten.

7.f) The reunion was moved to a banquet room **because the lodge was hosting its annual New Year's Eve party.**
Das Klassentreffen wurde in einen Bankettsaal verlegt, weil die Skihütte ihre jährliche Silvesterparty veranstaltete.

8.g) Brina stayed at the back of the room **so she could make a quiet exit just in case she felt like it.**
Brina blieb hinten im Raum, damit sie unbemerkt verschwinden könnte, falls ihr danach war.

46 **1.** When Brina walked into the reunion on the first night, she thought
[X] **Thomas was an underwear model a girl had hired to escort her.**
Als Brina am ersten Abend zum Klassentreffen ging, dachte sie, Thomas sei ein Unterwäschemodell, das eine junge Frau als Begleitung angeheuert hatte.

2. Brina thinks Thomas
[X] **looks like a guy who should always run around in his underwear.**
Brina findet, Thomas sieht aus wie ein Typ, der immer in Unterwäsche herumrennen sollte.

47 **1.** b) **to rather eat worms**
2. e) **to hold it in**
3. d) **to get carried away**
4. f) **to come up with something**
5. h) **to definitely want to find out**
6. g) **to keep a straight face**
7. c) **to pay attention**
8. a) **to talk yourself out of something**

48 **1.** The **more** Brina thought about it, the **angrier** she became.
2. Brina got an award for having changed the **most**.
3. Thomas had earned **a lot of** money before his thirtieth birthday.
4. Some of the guests were already **nearly** drunk.
5. The **less** she thought about Thomas, the **better** she'd feel.

49 **1.** Brina woke **late / later** that morning.
Brina erwachte spät / später am selben Morgen.
2. Thomas left a **telephone** message for Brina.
Thomas hinterließ Brina eine telefonische Nachricht.
3. He would be driving straight through to Denver and catching a plane **to** Palm Springs.
Er würde direkt nach Denver fahren und einen Flieger nach Palm Springs nehmen.
4. Brina called the front desk at **the hotel**.
Brina rief die Rezeption im Hotel an.
5. Then she headed **down the hall**.
Dann ging sie den Flur hinunter.
6. The maid cart was **inside Thomas's room**.
Der Wagen des Zimmermädchens stand in Thomas' Zimmer.
7. The furniture **had already been** polished by two maids.
Die Möbel waren von zwei Zimmermädchen bereits abgestaubt worden.

50 If she **asked** Mindy for Thomas's phone number, Mindy **would know** that he had not given Brina his address.
Wenn sie Mindy um Thomas' Telefonnummer bitten würde, dann wüsste Mindy, dass er Brina seine Adresse nicht gegeben hatte.

51 **1.** stare, see, **recognize**, watch, look
2. devour, drink, binge, **purge**, eat
3. toe, **thump**, wrist, knuckle, arm
4. pants, dress, top, **suite**, coat
5. purse, belt, **foot**, watch, shoes
6. **umbrella**, snow, ski, boots, lift
7. slide, glide, skid, **smooth**, stop
8. jealous, angry, embarrassed, mad, **loved**

Wörterverzeichnis

A.M.: 3 A.M. morgens, vormittags: 3 Uhr morgens
aback: to be (was/were – been) taken aback überrascht sein
abdomen Unterleib
about fast
about: to be (was/were – been) about to do something gerade etwas tun wollen
abrasion Reibung
abrasive reibend
accident Zufall
to ache schmerzen
aching schmerzhaft
across auf der anderen Seite
actually tatsächlich
ad Reklame
to adjust sich gewöhnen
to admit zugeben
advanced placement credits Anrechnung schulischer Leistungen im Studium
to afford sich leisten
agonized gequält
all but so gut wie
all-around allgemein
to amend sich korrigieren
amiable liebenswürdig
an effort at conversation Versuch, die Unterhaltung in Gang zu bringen
And raid it, they did. Und sie plünderten sie in der Tat.
Anglo angelsächsisch
ankle Knöchel
annoyed wütend
answering machine Anrufbeantworter
ant Ameise
anticipation Erwartung
any irgendein, irgendeine
anyway jedenfalls
to apologize sich entschuldigen
apparent augenscheinlich
appreciative bewundernd
to approach sich nähern
appropriate angebracht
aptly passend
to arch sich biegen
Are you embarrassed? Ist es dir peinlich?
to argue argumentieren
arousal Erregung
as hell verdammt
Aspen sehr populärer Wintersportort in den USA
ass over elbow Hals über Kopf
assault Angriff
to assemble sich versammeln
at an angle schräg
at the stroke of midnight Schlag Mitternacht
at the very least zumindest
to attend dabei sein
attendee Teilnehmende(r)

auburn rotbraun
to avoid vermeiden
awards ceremony Preisverleihung
aware: to be (was/were – been) aware of something sich einer Sache bewusst sein
awkward unsicher

babe magnet Frauenheld
to back down einen Rückzieher machen
back east im Osten
backdrop Hintergrund
badly sehr
bagel weiches, ringförmiges Brötchen
to ball up zusammenknüllen
ballsy mutig
bar Stange
bare nackt
to bargain for erwarten
bark Rinde
barrage Leuchtschwall
base layer Basisschicht
based mit (Firmen)Sitz
basic stuff Grundsätzliches
basket Teller (eines Skistocks)
bathroom stall Klokabine
to battle oneself mit sich kämpfen
to beat (beat – beaten) one's chest sich an die Brust schlagen
to beat the hell out of verdammt noch mal besser sein als
bed head: with bed head zerknautscht
beginner run Anfängerhügel
begrudgingly widerwillig
behind Hintern
belittling herabsetzend
to bend (bent – bent) beugen
beneath unter
to bet (bet – bet) wetten
to betray verraten
beyond über … hinweg
bill Schein; Rechnung
to binge sich vollstopfen
blank leer
bleary eyed mit trüben Augen
to blink zwinkern
blood pressure Blutdruck
to blow (blew – blown) someone off jemanden sausen lassen
to blow-dry föhnen
blown-up vergrößert
blubbering Flennen
blueprint Entwurf
to blurt out the truth mit der Wahrheit herausplatzen
to blush erröten
to boast prahlen
bold frech
boom Knall
to bother someone jemandem etwas ausmachen
to bother with a smile sich ein Lächeln abringen
bottom Hintern
bottom half untere Hälfte
bottom peg Fußstütze
bouquet Strauß
bow Kurve; Schleife
Boy Scout Pfadfinder
bra BH
to brace one's feet wide sich breitbeinig abstützen
braid Zopf
brain Hirn
to brave the cold der Kälte trotzen

to break (broke – broken) one's water die Fruchtblase zum Platzen bringen
to break up with somebody mit jemandem Schluss machen
breastbone Brustbein
breeze Brise
bridge of one's nose Nasenrücken
brief kurz
briefs Slip
brushed back zurückgeschoben
buck Dollar
to buckle zumachen; festschnallen
bud Knospe
buff fit
to build (built – built) up hochstilisieren
bullshit excuse windige Ausrede
bumper car Boxauto
bunch Haufen
to bunch sich zusammenziehen
bunny Häschen
bunny hill Idiotenhügel
buns Pobacken
bunting Fähnchen
bunting suit Strampelanzug
buried verborgen
burst Explosion
to burst (burst – burst) platzen
to bury verbergen, vergraben
to bust up laughing in Gelächter ausbrechen
but außer
butt Hintern; Zielscheibe
BVDs Unterhose (eigentlich der Name einer bekannten US-amerikanischen Unterhosen-Marke)

to care for gerne mögen
carnal sinnlich
carpet Teppich
carried: to get (got – got/gotten) carried away die Kontrolle verlieren
case Fall
casual lässig, leger, gelassen
casually lässig
cat track blau markierte Skipiste (für Anfänger), „Skiautobahn"
catch Kloß; Hauch
to catch (caught – caught) stecken bleiben
to catch a plane einen Flieger nehmen
to catch up on something etwas aufarbeiten, aufholen
ceiling Zimmerdecke
celebrity Berühmtheit
celery Sellerie
cell phone Handy
centerfold Nacktfotos auf der Doppelseite einer Sexzeitschrift
chandelier Kronleuchter
chapped rissig
charcoal dunkelgrau
charge Anspruch; Forderung
cheating case Fall von Betrug
to check prüfen
to check out testen; abkratzen
check-for-drool devastating zum Sabbern umwerfend
cheeks of one's behind Pobacken
chef Koch
chess club Schachklub
chest Brustkorb
chin Kinn

to chirp zwitschern
chocolate-covered in Schokolade gehüllt
to chuckle in sich hinein lachen
chunky klobig
to cinch in at the waist auf Taille arbeiten
Cinderella Aschenputtel
city council meeting Stadtratsversammlung
to claim einfordern
claimant Antragsteller(in)
clasp Nadel, Haken
to clear sich entfernen
clearing Lichtung
cleavage Ausschnitt
cleft Spalte
to climax zum Höhepunkt kommen
climax Höhepunkt
to cling (clung – clung) hängen
to clog verstopfen
close kurz davor
closed-up verschlossen
closet Kleiderschrank
closure Verschluss
clue Ahnung
to clutch umklammern
collar Kragen
to comb kämmen
to come (came – come) up with something auf etwas kommen
command Herrschaft
complete völlig
complimentary gratis
to conceal verbergen
concerned: where you're concerned was dich betrifft
conclusion Schlussfolgerung
condo Eigentumswohnung
confined: to be (was/were – been) confined to a wheelchair an den Rollstuhl gefesselt sein
confusion Verwirrung
connected verbunden
connection innere Verbindung
to consist of bestehen aus
consultant Berater
consultant work beratende Tätigkeit
to consume beherrschen
contour Umriss
to contract sich verengen
to converge zusammentreffen
cookie Keks
coordinated koordiniert
corkscrew Korkenzieher
corrugated gewellt
to course fließen
court order richterliche Verfügung
to cover bedecken
cozy behaglich
to crack a joke einen Witz reißen
crackle Knistern
to crank out produzieren
crappy mood miese Laune
to crash ins Bett fallen
to crave begehren
crease Fältchen
creek Bach
to creep (crept – crept) kriechen
to crinkle in Fältchen legen
crisp kalt
crop Gruppe
to cross kreuzen
crotch Unterleib
to crunch knacken
crunch Knirschen
crushed: to be (was/were – been) crushed am Boden zerstört sein

to cup umschließen
cup size Körbchengröße (des BHs)
cured gepökelt
curious neugierig
to curl wirbeln, sich kräuseln, sich wickeln
curl Locke
current Strom
currently zurzeit
curtains Vorhänge
to curve to schwenken nach
cut-crystal glass Kristallglas
cute süß, niedlich

damask Damast
damp feucht
dash (dashboard) Armaturenbrett
death cookie großer Brocken aus hartem Schnee
decent anständig
deck Terrasse
to degrade someone jemanden erniedrigen
delicious köstlich
delusion Täuschung
dense growth dichter Wuchs
to depend: (That) Depends. Kommt drauf an.
to deserve verdienen
desire Sehnsucht
desk Schreibtisch
despite trotz
deteriorated vergammelt
to devour verschlingen
to dial wählen
to die nachlassen
to dig (dug – dug) graben
to dip sich neigen
to direct führen
directionless ziellos
dirt-poor bettelarm
disappointment Enttäuschung
to discard verwerfen
disease Krankheit
to dismiss verdrängen
display Anblick
to disturb unterbrechen
disturbing beunruhigend
to divert one's attention sich ablenken
divorced geschieden
to do (did – done) for a living sein Geld verdienen
to do in fertigmachen
to dodge ausweichen
doll Puppe
Donald Trump US-amerikanischer Milliardär
doofus Doofi
dork Idiot(in)
dorky dämlich
double major doppelter Studienabschluss
downhill Abfahrt
to drag oneself sich schleppen
dragged: to be (was/were – been) dragged aufsteigen
dragonfly Libelle
to drain leeren
Drained of … Ganz ohne …
to draw (drew – drawn) einnehmen
to draw upon saugen an
to dress left Linksträger sein
to drift shut sich schließen
to drive (drove – driven) into eindringen in
driveway Einfahrt
to drop sinken lassen

to drop off abliefern, absetzen
droplet Tröpfchen
to drown out übertönen
drugged wie unter Drogen
drugstore Drogerie
drunken betrunken
to dump fallen lassen
to dwindle sich auflösen
dyed gefärbt
dying: to be (was/were – been) dying to know unbedingt wissen wollen
Dynastar Marke für Skiartikel

earlier vorhin
to ease gleiten; sanft an sich drücken
easel Staffelei
Easter Bunny Osterhase
easygoing unkompliziert
to eat (ate – eaten) at nagen an
eclipsed übertroffen
edge Rand, Kante
effort Anstrengung
effortlessly mühelos
elastic band Gummiband
Elle Macpherson Fotomodell und Schauspielerin aus Australien
elongated länglich
embarrassment Verlegenheit
embossed geprägt
embrace Umarmung
embroidered gestickt
emphasis Verstärkung
to encourage ermutigen
energetic energisch
engine Motor
engorged prall
to enjoy oneself Spaß machen
to enter: It had never entered his head. Es war ihm nie in den Sinn gekommen.
to entertain unterhalten
enthusiasm Begeisterung
to entwine einander umschlingen
equally genauso
equipment Skiausrüstung
ermine Hermelin
erratic unregelmäßig
etched geformt
eternally ewig
eventually eines Tages
to evolve sich weiterentwickeln
exaggeration Übertreibung
except for außer
exhalation Ausatmen
exhausted erschöpft
to expand sich weiten
to explore erforschen
expressionless ausdruckslos

fabric Textil
to fail es nicht schaffen
fairly ziemlich
to fall (fell – fallen) for sich verlieben in
to fall for it darauf hereinfallen
to fall in love with sich verlieben in
familiar vertraut
far side Rückseite
farther weiter
fashion statement: to be (was/were – been) a great fashion statement supermodern sein
to feast on verschlingen
features Gesichtszüge

to feed (fed – fed) off verschlingen
to feel (felt – felt) the way sich so fühlen wie
to feel clueless keine Ahnung haben
fence Zaun
to figure davon ausgehen
to figure something out etwas herausfinden
files Unterlagen
to fill out Kurven bekommen
filling sättigend
first off erstens
to fit (fit – fit) passen
to fit the bed with new sheets das Bett beziehen
five foot seven ein Meter siebzig
five-inch heels Pumps mit 12 cm hohen Absätzen
flagrant offenkundig
to flash blitzen, flackern, blinken
flat eiskalt
flaw Fehler
flawless makellos
flesh Fleisch
to flex sich anspannen
to flicker flackern
to fling (flung – flung) achtlos werfen
to flip schnellen (lassen)
to flip aside beiseite schieben
to flip up hochheben
floor Fußboden
floorboard Bodenbrett
fluid flüssig
flush Erröten
fluted glass Sektglas
to flutter flattern, flackern
focus: to be (was/were – been) focused on sich konzentrieren auf
to fold against one's chest an die Brust drücken
folder Ordner
foot Fuß (Längenmaß: 0,3048 m)
for so long eine ganze Weile lang
for themselves ihrer selbst wegen
forearm Unterarm
forehead Stirn
forest service Forstverwaltung
four-poster bed Himmelbett
fraction Spur
fractured gebrochen
fragrance Duft
frankly ehrlich gesagt
frantically voller Panik
fraud Betrug
freaky irre
freckles Sommersprossen
free kostenlos
to freeze (froze – frozen) off abfrieren
friction burn Reibungswunde
frigid eisig
front yard Vorgarten
front-row in der ersten Reihe
to frown die Stirn runzeln
full-blown richtig
full-fledged richtig
funeral Beerdigung
furrow Furche
future heir zukünftiger Erbe

to gain zunehmen
gangly schlaksig
to gasp keuchen
gate Tor
to gather sich sammeln
gay schwul

gear Ausrüstung
Gee! Meine Güte!
geek Computerfreak
gentle sanft
genuinely aufrichtig
to get (got – got/gotten) over hinwegkommen über
Get out (of here)! Red keinen Unsinn!
to get stuck stecken bleiben
to get the wind knocked out of one jemandem den Atem verschlagen
gift Geschenk
to give (gave – given) birth entbinden
to give nothing away nichts verraten
to give someone a hard time jemandem das Leben schwer machen
gladly nur zu gern
to glance up aufsehen
glassy glasig
gloved im Handschuh steckend
to go (went – gone) about something etwas angehen
to go after sich nehmen
to go public an die Börse gehen
to go toe to toe with somebody jemandem gegenübertreten
goal Ziel
goat position Ziegenstellung
God forbid! Gott behüte!
goggles Skibrille
goody super
gorgeous umwerfend
to grab packen
to grab ahold of something etwas packen
graceful graziös
gracious liebenswürdig
grade school Grundschule
to graduate den höheren Schulabschluss der Highschool machen
graduating class Abschlussklasse
to grapple kämpfen
grateful dankbar
to graze streifen
greed Gier
to grind (ground – ground) sich reiben
to grip packen
groan Stöhnen
groin Leistengegend
growing streak Wachstumsschub
guaranteed: to be (was/were – been) guaranteed to survive a nuclear holocaust garantiert einen Atomangriff überstehen
to guess right es erraten
guilty schuldig
to gun for verfolgen

halfway halb
hall Flur
to hand überreichen
handsome gut aussehend
to hang (hung – hung) back hinten bleiben
to hang on to the hope sich an die Hoffnung klammern
to hang out rumhängen, Zeit verbringen
hangover Kater (nach Alkoholrausch)

hard: to be (was/were – been) too hard on oneself zu streng mit sich umgehen
harsh scharf
hasty übereilt
to have (had – had) a crush on someone in jemanden verknallt sein
to have in mind sich vorstellen
have: the haves and have-nots die Reichen und die Armen
hazel haselnussbraun
head Eichel
head Haupt-
to head for sich auf den Weg machen zu
to head straight for something direkt zu etwas übergehen
headboard Kopfteil
headed: to be (was/were – been) headed gehen
header Köpfer
heart palpitations Herzklopfen
heavy drapery schwerer Vorhang
Heck no! Himmel nein!
heel Absatz
to help: He couldn't help but … Er konnte nicht umhin …
to herd cattle Vieh zusammentreiben
high heels Pumps
hint Andeutung
hip pocket Hosentasche
to hire beauftragen
to hit (hit – hit) besuchen; drücken auf; schlagen gegen
to hit the jackpot das große Los ziehen
to hitch stecken bleiben
to hold (held – held) one's breath den Atem anhalten
to hold in sich zurückhalten
holder Spange
hollow hohl; Einbuchtung
Holy shit! Du liebe Scheiße!
Home Ec Club Hauswirtschafts-AG
homemaker Hausfrau
to hook anschließen, stecken
to hook up with sich zusammentun mit
hooker Nutte
hoop ringförmiger Ohrring
to host geben
hot shivers heiße Schauer
to hover schweben
to hover around thirty degrees sich um den Gefrierpunkt halten (30° F = ca. -1° C)
to hug: It hugged her curves. Es schmiegte sich an ihre Rundungen.
Hugh Hefner Erfinder und Herausgeber des Magazins „Playboy"
humiliation Demütigung
hunk Brocken
hunky muskulös
to hunt witches Hexen jagen
hushed gedämpft

I guess not. Wohl nicht.
to imagine sich vorstellen
immediately sofort
impeccable makellos
to imply suggerieren
to impress beeindrucken
to improve besser werden
in common gemeinsam

in favor of zugunsten
in the context of im Zusammenhang mit
in the least ganz und gar nicht
in unison einstimmig
inch Zoll (= 2,54 cm)
incline Neigung
including einschließlich
incredible unglaublich
index finger Zeigefinger
to inhale einatmen
innocent unschuldig
insane verrückt
inside out verkehrt herum
insides Inneres
insincere unaufrichtig
insistent beharrlich
instantly sofort
to instruct instruieren
insurance fraud Versicherungsbetrug
intense intensiv
intention Absicht
interest Anteil
inward nach innen
itinerary Programm

to jab stechen
Jacuzzi Whirlpool
jaw Kiefer
jealousy Eifersucht
Jeez! Mensch!
to jerk reißen
jerk Idiot(in)
to join sich anschließen
joke Witz
to judge beurteilen
juicy schlüpfrig
to jump poppen
junior high school Mittelschule
just above a whisper kaum lauter als ein Flüstern
to jut zeigen

Kathy Ireland Fotomodell und Schauspielerin aus den USA
to keep (kept – kept) from sliding nicht abrutschen
to keep oneself occupied sich ablenken
to keep someone company jemandem Gesellschaft leisten
to kick-start neu starten
kid Junge
to kid oneself sich vormachen
kiss-my-ass du-kannst-mich-mal
to kneel (knelt – knelt) sich hinknien
knobby knubbelig
to knock flat am Boden zerstört zurücklassen
knuckle Fingerknöchel
kohl pencil Kajalstift

lab Labor
Lab Labrador
lace panties Spitzenhöschen
lame lahm
lanky schlaksig
to lapse abdriften, verfallen
larger than life überlebensgroß
lash Wimper
to last halten
late bloomer Spätentwickler(in)
latte Milchkaffee

laundry Schmutzwäsche
layer Schicht
to leap (leaped/leapt – leaped/leapt): Her heart leapt. Ihr Herz schlug höher.
to leave (left – left) abfahren; lassen
to let (let – let) go of loslassen
liar Lügner(in)
license plate number Kennzeichen
lid Lid
to lie lügen
lift line Lift-Schlange
to light (lit – lit) erhellen
lime slice Limettenscheibe
linen Leinen
to linger verharren
lingerie Unterwäsche
liquid flüssig
local hiesig
to locate finden
locked verschmolzen
lodge Ferienhotel
loner Einzelgänger(in)
long johns lange Unterhosen
to long to hear hören wollen
longing Sehnsucht
to look down one's nose (at someone) auf jemanden herabsehen
to look pathetic lächerlich wirken
loose locker
to lose (lost – lost) one's mind den Verstand verlieren
lost: to be (was/were – been) lost on someone an jemandem verschwendet sein
lousy lay schlecht im Bett
to love: I'd love for you to see it ich möchte gern, dass du es siehst
low fat fettarm
lucky: to be (was/were – been) lucky Glück haben
lump Kloß
lust Verlangen

mad sauer, wütend
maid cart Wagen des Zimmermädchens
major Hauptfach im Studium
to make (made – made) a beeline schnurstracks gehen
to make a grab for packen
to make a quiet exit unbemerkt verschwinden
to make an effort sich Mühe geben
to make inquiries Nachforschungen anstellen
to make it big es zu etwas bringen
to make it up es wieder gutmachen
to make love to somebody mit jemandem schlafen
to make money Geld verdienen
to make the Fortune 500 auf die Liste der 500 größten US-amerikanischen Unternehmen kommen (erstellt vom Fortune Magazine)
to make up for aufholen
Malibu schicker Badeort in Kalifornien
market shares Marktanteile
match head Streichholzkopf
material Stoff
meadow Wiese
mean gemein
to mean (meant – meant) it es ernst meinen
meaningless belanglos
mechanic Automechaniker(in)

medical care ärztliche Versorgung
to meet (met – met) someone's gaze jemandem in die Augen schauen
to melt schmelzen, zum Schmelzen bringen
member Mitglied
merely einfach nur
mess Durcheinander
message Nachricht
to mind: he didn't mind es hat ihm nichts ausgemacht
to mingle sich (ver)mischen
mirrored ball Spiegelkugel
to misconstrue missverstehen
to misinterpret missverstehen
to mistake (mistook – mistaken) falsch verstehen
to moan stöhnen
mock T-neck Top mit Stehkragen
mogul Buckel
moisture Feuchtigkeit
to mold formen
moldy fad
more like schon eher
morning breath Mundgeruch
moron Idiot(in)
mounted montiert
munchkin Zwerg
muscle car Coupé oder Cabrio mit PS-starkem Motor
musk Moschus
musky moschusartig

nagging nagend
to name aussuchen
name tag Namensschild
napkin Papierserviette
to narrow sich verengen
near fast
nearly annähernd
need Verlangen
nerd Langweiler(in)
netting Netz
New Year's Eve celebration Silvesterparty
to nibble one's way sich vorknabbern
nightmare Albtraum
ninth grade neunte Klasse
to nip beißen
nipple Brustwarze
no big deal keine große Sache
no way auf keinen Fall
noon Mittag
nope nee
notice Ankündigung
noticeable spürbar
NRA (National Rifle Association) Waffenlobby in den USA
nurse Krankenschwester

to object to ablehnen
okay: to be (was/were – been) okay by oneself selbst genug vorweisen können
on the road auf Tour
one way or the other so oder so
one-piece Einteiler
onslaught Angriff
opportunity Chance
oral pleasure Oralsex
ounce Unze
outcast Außenseiter(in)
to outdo (outdid – outdone) übertreffen
to outline sich abzeichnen

outline Umriss
outskirts Stadtrand
over and over immer wieder
to overlook überblicken
overly allzu
overstuffed zu prall gepolstert
overwhelming überwältigend
to owe schulden
ownership Besitzrechte

P.M.: 10:30 P.M. nachmittags, abends: 22.30 Uhr
to pack on zunehmen
packed überfüllt
packed powder Pulverschnee
pad Ballen
palm Handfläche
paragraph Abschnitt
parking lot Parkplatz
parking slot Parklücke
to part sich öffnen
particular bestimmt
partyer Partygast
passion Leidenschaft
passionate leidenschaftlich
to pay zahlen
to pay attention aufpassen
to pay off sich auszahlen
peacoat Caban (Wolljacke im Stil der Marine)
pelvis Becken
pep club Anfeuerungsklub (ähnlich wie Cheerleaders)
perimeter Peripherie
perky: in a perky sort of way auf lebhafte Art
permission Erlaubnis
to persuade überreden
pervert Perverse(r)
to phrase ausdrücken
Picabo Street US-amerikanische Skirennläuferin
to pick up speed schneller werden
to pick up the pieces die Scherben aufsammeln
picky wählerisch
to picture sich vorstellen
pillow Kopfkissen
to pin pressen, anstecken
pinch Zwicken
pine Kiefer
to pitch fallen
pitched getaucht
to place legen
to plant (in den Schnee) stecken
plates Kennzeichen
to plead sich berufen auf; betteln
pleasurable angenehm
pleasure Spaß
pleezze bitte, bitte
to plummet sinken
to plunge eintauchen
to point ausrichten
point Spitze
to poke stoßen (gegen); stechen
polish Nagellack
to polish off leeren (Getränk)
pond Teich
ponytail Pferdeschwanz
pool Gruppe
to pop einwerfen
to pop out hervorbringen
Popsicle Eis am Stiel
Postum Ersatzkaffee aus Getreide
to pound hämmern
to pour eingießen, fließen, strömen
powder Puder
to prank einen Streich spielen

to pray beten
to predict voraussagen
to prefer vorziehen
preprogrammed vorprogrammiert
to pretend so tun als
pride Stolz
primal animalisch
prism Prisma
private investigator Privatdetektiv(in)
prize Preis
pro Profi-
prolonged ausgedehnt
prom Schulball
promiscuous sexuell freizügig
to provide sorgen für
to provide for a child für ein Kind sorgen
provided serviert
proximity Nähe
prude prüder Mensch
pubic hair Schamhaar
public rest room öffentliche Toilette
to pucker sich spitzen
puckered gekräuselt
pudgy pummelig
to pull at zerren an
pull string Zugschnur
to pull up to bis … fahren
to pump bewegen
to punch schlagen
pure rein
to purge sich reinigen
purposely bewusst, absichtlich
purse Handtasche
pursuing das Jagen
to put (put – put): She was to put him through. Sie sollte ihn durchstellen.
to put directly through direkt durchstellen

qualm Skrupel
quarterback Spielmacher (im American Football)
quiet Stille
to quit (quit – quit) kündigen

to race up rasen
ragged chaotisch
rah-rah ausgelassen
to raid plündern
railing Geländer
ramp Rampe
to rank right up with something einer Sache gleichkommen
rather lieber
to reach erreichen
to reach for greifen nach
to read (read – read) into hineininterpretieren in
reassurance Bestätigung
to recall sich erinnern
receiver Hörer
to recognize erkennen
to refer to sich beziehen auf
reflection Spiegelbild
registration desk Rezeption
registration form Anmeldeformular
to reintroduce wieder vorstellen
Reliant britische Automarke, meist Dreiradfahrzeuge
relieved: to be (was/were – been) relieved erleichtert sein
reluctant: to be (was/were – been) reluctant to do something sich sträuben, etwas zu tun

to remind someone jemanden erinnern
reminder Gedächtnisstütze
rendering Version
to rent leihen
reproductive organ Geschlechtsorgan
resemblance Ähnlichkeit
to resemble ähneln, wirken wie
resort (town) Ferienort
to respond reagieren
to restock wieder auffüllen
restraint Beherrschung
to retreat sich zurückziehen
to retrieve holen
reunion Klassentreffen
to revert to zurückkehren zu
to revolve around sich drehen um
revolving door Drehtür
Richard Simmons US-amerikanischer Fitness-Guru
rim Rand
to ring (rang – rung) in einläuten
riotous aufständisch
to rip reißen
to rip off wegreißen
to rip one's heart out einem das Herz brechen
to rise (rose – risen) onto one's toes sich auf die Zehenspitzen stellen
roaring lodernd
to rob someone of breath jemandem den Atem rauben
robe Morgenmantel
to rock back on one's heels das Gewicht auf die Fersen verlagern
rocket Rakete
rockhard steinhart
to roll around kreisen
roller coaster Achterbahn
to romp around like a goat wie eine Ziege herumtollen
Rose Garden Multifunktionsarena in Portland, Oregon
to rot verfaulen
rough rau
to round up zusammentragen
rug rat Hosenscheißer
rumor Gerücht
to run (ran – run) through the instructions die Anleitung durchgehen
Rupert Everett britischer Schauspieler und Sänger

sacred heilig
safety bar Sicherheitsbügel
Sally Jessy populäre Talkshow im US-Fernsehen mit Sally Jessy Raphael als Gastgeberin
sanity Vernunft
saying Spruch
to scan durchsuchen
to scare: it scares me shitless ich mache mir vor Angst in die Hose
scent Duft
schnapps Schnaps
scholarship Stipendium
to scoop up hochheben
screen Bildschirm
sculpted wie gemeißelt
to seal versiegeln
to search suchen
Sears US-amerikanisches Großversandhaus
to seduce verführen; locken
to see (saw – seen) someone mit jemandem zusammen sein

self-consciousness Befangenheit
semblance Anschein
semierect halb erigiert
seminal bead Samentropfen
sensation Gefühl
sense Sinn
sensitive einfühlsam, empfindlich
sensual sinnlich
serious: to be (was/were – been) serious es ernst meinen
to set (set – set) untergehen
to set off veranstalten
sewn aufgenäht
shade Schattierung
shades Sonnenbrille
shaft Schaft; Strahlen
to shake (shook – shaken) the ground den Boden erzittern lassen
shaky zitternd
shallow oberflächlich
shame: It's a shame. Das ist schade.
shareholder Aktionär(in)
She didn't care. Es war ihr egal.
shearling boots Fellstiefel
sheer hauchdünn
sheets: to be (was/were – been) well past three sheets schon viel zu tief ins Glas geschaut haben
to shift sich bewegen
shiver Schauer
to shoot (shot – shot) past something an etwas vorbeirasen
shortly kurz darauf
short-sleeved kurzärmelig
shot Spritze
to shove stecken, stoßen
to shove the vehicle into gear einen Gang einlegen
to shove the vehicle into park den Schalthebel (des Fahrzeugs) auf „Parken“ schieben
show and tell zeigen und erläutern
to shrug mit den Achseln zucken
shudder Schaudern
to shut (shut – shut) schließen
shut down ausgestorben
silently stumm
silk Seide
silk purse Seidentäschchen
sill Sims
since da, weil
sincere aufrichtig
sip Schluck
to sit (sat – sat) parked parken
ski bum Skifreak
ski patrol Pistenrettung
ski pole Skistock
ski run Skipiste
to skid schlittern
to skid to a stop stehen bleiben
to skim wandern lassen
skinny dürr
skintight hauteng
skirt Rock
to slam shut zuschlagen
to slice schneiden
slick glatt
to slide (slid – slid) gleiten, gleiten lassen; schieben
to slide into geraten zu
to slide off abrutschen
slight leicht
slit Schlitz
slumberous schläfrig
smooth glatt, weich; süffig
to snap one's fingers mit den Fingern schnippen
to sneak off sich davonstehlen

snowcapped schneebedeckt
So what was new? Wie üblich.
softly sanft
solar flare Sonneneruption
solid: the solid wall of his chest sein fester Brustkorb
some: That was some outfit! Das war vielleicht ein Outfit!
something: There was something about her. Es war etwas Besonderes an ihr.
sophomore Student(in) im zweiten Studienjahr
sore weh
southern states Südstaaten
to spare schenken
spark Funke
sparkling glitzernd
speaker Lautsprecher
spear Speer
to speed (speeded/sped – speeded/sped) up beschleunigen
to spike antreiben
to spill (spilled/spilt – spilled/spilt) verschütten
spine Wirbelsäule
split second Bruchteil einer Sekunde
to spot entdecken
spouse Ehepartner(in)
spread Überwurf
to spread (spread – spread) kriechen, spreizen
to spread out ausbreiten
to sprinkle streuen
to spy entdecken
to squeeze drücken
squiggly schnörkelig
to squint spähen
to stab stechen
stage Phase
to stall zögern
Stanley Cup Trophäe im Eishockey
stark krass
starstruck vom Ruhm geblendet
to start gründen
to startle erschrecken
to stay on draufbleiben
to steer steuern
step Stufe
stereo Stereoanlage
sternum Brustbein
stiff steif
to still zur Ruhe bringen
to sting (stung – stung) brennen
to stir aufwirbeln
stock Aktien
stocked gefüllt
stoic gelassen
to stop dead abrupt hängen bleiben
stored gespeichert
to straddle sich rittlings setzen
straight hetero; geradewegs
strained mitgenommen
strains Melodie
strap Riemen, Gurt, Schlaufen
streamer Luftschlange
to stretch ausbreiten
strewn verstreut
stride Schritt
to strike (struck – struck) up einsetzen mit
to string (strung – strung) up aufhängen
stroke Streicheln
to stroke streicheln
to stroll schlendern
to study mustern
Stun Master Elektroschocker
stunned geschockt
sub shop Sandwichbar

subtle subtil
to suck ätzend sein; saugen an
to suck away schwächen
to suck in einsaugen
to suck in one's breath hörbar einatmen
suction Sog
suede Wildleder
to suffer leiden
supposed: to be (was/were – been) supposed to do something etwas tun sollen
supposedly angeblich
surgical supplies Operationszubehör
surrounded umringt
suspicion Verdacht
to swallow up schlucken
swarthy dunkelhäutig
swathed überhäuft
to swear (swore – sworn) fluchen
sweater Pulli
sweep Schwingen
to sweep (swept – swept) streichen
sweetheart Freund
swell Wölbung
swimsuit bottoms Bikinihöschen
to swing (swung- swung) schwingen
to swirl sprudeln
to swish sausen
switch Schalter
sworn in vereidigt

tab Schiebegriff (am Reißverschluss)
tailored zugeschnitten
tailoring Schnitt
tails Enden
to take (took – taken) advantage ausnützen
to take offense übel nehmen
to take one's mind off something nicht mehr an etwas denken
to take state die Bundesstaatsmeisterschaften gewinnen
to take time off sich freinehmen
to talk oneself out of something sich etwas ausreden
tamed gezähmt
tan gebräunt
tangle Knäuel
to tangle sich verheddern
taste Geschmack
to tear (tore – torn) entfahren
to tear off wegreißen
tear-off-my-clothes reiß-mir-die-Kleider-vom-Leib
teasing neckend
telephone directory Telefonbuch
temple Schläfe
tempted: to be (was/were – been) tempted to do something versucht sein etwas zu tun
tenacious hartnäckig
tension Anspannung
texture Konsistenz
the … the je … desto
the latter der (die, das) Letztere
the least am wenigsten
the remaining one der übrige
the second in dem Moment
the small of one's back das Kreuz
the very center genau in der Mitte
the wait das Warten
the worst das Schlimmste
theater Kino

There was no mistaking … Es war eindeutig …
There was no mistaking … for …. Man konnte … nicht mit … verwechseln.
There was no use … Es war sinnlos …
thigh Oberschenkel
third floor 2. Stock (American English); 3. Stock (British English)
threat Bedrohung
throng Gedränge
to thrust (thrust – thrust) stoßen
thud Klopfen
to thump schlagen
to thump and tune herumtrommeln und die Instrumente stimmen
thwarted gehindert
to tickle kitzeln
tie: The bet is a tie. Die Wette ist unentschieden.
tight dicht
to tighten sich straffen; den Druck verstärken
to tilt schräg legen
tilt Verziehen
timber Holz
tin Dose
tingle Kribbeln
tinted getönt
tip Spitze
tiptoes Zehenspitzen
T-neck Rolli
toenail Zehennagel
tongue Zunge
tonsils (Rachen)Mandeln
to torment quälen
to torture quälen
to toss werfen
towel Handtuch
towering hoch
town Kleinstadt
trace Spur
to trace entlangfahren
to trace missing people Vermisste aufspüren
track Kante
to track someone down jemanden finden
Trail Blazers Basketball-Profimannschaft in Portland, Oregon
trail marker Hangmarkierung
tramp Landstreicher(in)
trapped: to get (got – got/gotten) trapped hängen bleiben
treasure trove Schatzkammer
tree fort Baumfestung
to trip stolpern
to trip down memory lane in Erinnerungen schwelgen
trombonist Posaunist(in)
trophy Trophäe
trophy cup Pokal
to tuck into in … stopfen
tug Ruck
to tug ziehen, zerren
tummy Bauch
turn Kurve
to turn on anmachen
to turn up hochklappen
turned upside down auf den Kopf gestellt
turtleneck Rollkragenpulli
tuxedo Smoking
twinge Spur
twist Drehung
to twist around umwickeln
to twist somebody into a confused knot jemanden völlig durcheinander und verwirrt machen
two-story zweistöckig

ugly hässlich
uh huh mmh
umbrella Schirm
to unbraid entflechten
uncomfortable unangenehm
undergrowth Gestrüpp
unemployed arbeitslos
uneven rau
unexpected unerwartet
unibrow zusammengewachsene Augenbrauen
to unlock lösen
unrepentant reuelos
unruly widerspenstig
unsteady unsicher
uptight verklemmt, verkrampft
to use someone jemanden benutzen
to utter hervorstoßen
utterly vollkommen

to vacuum (staub)saugen
vein Ader
virginity Unschuld
virtually praktisch
visceral instinktiv
volley Salve
to vow schwören, sich schwören

Wagoneer Typ von Geländewagen
waistband Bund
to wait one's turn warten bis man an der Reihe ist
waiter Kellner
to walk about herumlaufen
wanna (= Do you want to ...?) willste
warped abartig
to water tränen
wavy gewellt
way too much viel zu viel
to weave (wove – woven) flechten, sich schlängeln
to weave one's way sich seinen Weg bahnen
wedge Schneepflug (Schwung beim Skifahren)
wedgies Keilabsätze
weeny Weichei
to weigh wiegen
weight Gewicht
what in (the) hell was zum Teufel
what kind of (money) wie viel (Geld)
whenever wann immer
wherever wo immer
to whip around herumwirbeln
whoever wer auch immer
to whoosh zischen
whopping gigantisch
wife Ehefrau
willing bereit
wimpy erbärmlich
to wind (wound – wound) schlingen
to wind one's way sich durchzwängen
windshield Windschutzscheibe
to withdraw (withdrew – withdrawn) sich zurückziehen
within in
without budging ohne sich von der Stelle zu bewegen
witty geistreich

to work the lather through one's hair den Schaum ins Haar einmassieren
workmen's compensation claim Schadensersatz für einen Arbeitsunfall
worm Wurm
worried beunruhigt
to worry about something sich um etwas Sorgen machen
to worship anbeten
worth one's time lohnenswert
worth: it was worth the wait das Warten hat sich gelohnt
wrinkle Falte
wrong: to be (was/were – been) wrong sich irren

to yawn gähnen
to yearn sich sehnen
yep ja
yesterday's garbage Müll von gestern
You're kidding! Das kannst du nicht ernst meinen!
to yuck it up Witze reißen

to zap elektrisieren
to zip up einen Reißverschluss haben